Southwestern
BAPTIST THEOLOGICAL SEMINARY

D6®

FAMILY MINISTRY Journal

VOLUME 5

RANDALL HOUSE
ACADEMIC

Printed in the United States of America

ISBN 9781614841586

Manuscript submission
Intent to submit, including topic and abstract should be emailed by June 1 to the managing editor at journal.editor@d6family.com. Authors will be notified of acceptance. Research articles will be peer-reviewed, and accepted papers will be included in the print issue, which is released in the spring at the D6 Conference.

Word count: academic research articles (3,000–5,000 words), practitioner essays (1,000 words), book reviews (800 words max.).

If you are interested in participating as a peer reviewer in the double-blind peer-review process for the research articles, email journal.editor@d6family.com.

Purpose Statement

The purpose of the *Southwestern D6 Family Ministry Journal* is to support the thinking and practices of parenting in Christian homes, in family ministry in the local church, and in parachurch settings that reflect God's intent for generational discipleship as presented in Deuteronomy 6 and other biblical texts. This purpose is achieved by the publication of articles and essays that do the following:

- Reflect on the scriptural foundations of God's use of paternal and maternal influences in the lives of children and grandchildren while also acknowledging various contemporary family situations
- Explore the integration and application of the relationship between the church and home
- Support the teaching of generational approaches to Christian education at colleges and seminaries for the equipping of ministry leaders and parents
- Champion methodologies that prepare children and young adults in the development of a Christian lifestyle and Christian leadership skills

The journal is primarily intended for two audiences: an academic community of professors and students in institutions of higher learning who are committed to the development of a new generation of Christian ministers and community leaders. Second, those professionals who are already serving in local church and parachurch settings. In order to facilitate discussion and learning among both groups, each publication will:

- Provide publishing opportunities primarily for:
    - academic peer reviewed work
    - practitioner reflection
- Offer a platform for research into family ministry
- Review new books connected to generational discipleship and classic texts in family ministry related fields

Southwestern D6 Family Ministry Journal Doctrine Statement

1. We believe the Bible to be the inspired, infallible, inerrant, only authoritative Word of God (Romans 15:4; 2 Timothy 3:15–17; Hebrews 4:12; 1 Peter 1:25; 2 Peter 1:19–21).
2. We believe there is one God, eternally existent in three persons: Father, Son, and Holy Spirit (Genesis 1:1–2; Deuteronomy 6:4; Psalm 90:2; Isaiah 40:28; Matthew 3:16–17; 28:19; John 1:1–3; 10:29–30; 14:9–11; 1 Corinthians 8:6; 2 Corinthians 3:17; 13:14; Ephesians 4:4–6; Colossians 1:15–17; 2:9; 1 Timothy 1:17; 1 Peter 1:1–2; Hebrews 9:14).
3. We believe in the deity of our Lord Jesus Christ, in His virgin birth, in His bodily resurrection, in His ascension to the right hand of the Father, and in His personal return in power and glory (Matthew 1:18–23; John 1:1–18; 8:58; Acts 1:9–11; 1 Corinthians 15:1–8; Colossians 1:13–22; 2:9; 1 Timothy 3:16; Hebrews 1:3).
4. We believe in the present ministry of the Holy Spirit by whose indwelling the Christian is enabled to live a godly life (John 14:16–17; 16:7–14; Romans 8:9–11; Ephesians 1:13–14; Titus 3:4–7; Hebrews 9:14).
5. We believe God created all people in His own image. Scripture teaches that God created them male and female. Gender is a gift and is part of God's good creation (Genesis 1:26–27; 2:18–25; Matthew 19:4–6).
6. We believe the first man and woman—Adam and Eve—sinned against God (Genesis 3:1–24). Scripture teaches, "Sin came into the world through one man, and death through sin, and so death spread to all men because all sinned" (Romans 5:12). We believe God loves us, even in our sin, and has demonstrated his love for us by sending His Son, Jesus Christ. As Scripture teaches, "God shows his love for us in that while we were still sinners, Christ died for us" (Romans 5:8).
7. We believe salvation comes by grace through faith in Jesus Christ, who died on the cross, was buried for three days, and rose again (Ephesians 2:8–9; 1 Corinthians 15:3–5). Salvation brings redemption to the whole person and guarantees eternal life (Ephesians 1:3–14; 2 Corinthians 5:17). Salvation includes regeneration, justification, sanctification, and glorification (Romans 8:30). Salvation is only found through faith in Jesus Christ as Lord: "And there is salvation in no one else, for there is no other name under heaven given among men by which we must be saved" (Acts 4:12).
8. We believe in the resurrection of both the saved and the lost; they that are saved unto the resurrection of life and they that are lost unto the resurrection of damnation (Matthew 25:46; John 3:16; 11:25–26; Romans 6:23; 14:10; Philippians 3:20–21; 1 Thessalonians 4:14–18; 2 Thessalonians 1:5–10; Hebrews 9:27–28).
9. We believe in the spiritual unity of believers in our Lord Jesus Christ (John 17:20–23; 1 Corinthians 1:10; Galatians 3:28; Ephesians 2:11–22; 4:3–6; Philippians 2:2).
10. We believe God created marriage and family (Genesis 2:18–25; Matthew 19:4–6). Family consists of those related by marriage, blood, or adoption. Marriage is between

one man and one woman who come together as one flesh in a lifelong, covenant commitment. The husband and wife are of equal worth and are both made in the image of God. Wives are to submit to their own husbands and husbands are to love their wives as Christ loved the church (Ephesians 5:22, 25). We believe children are a blessing from the Lord (Psalm 127:3), and parents are commanded to teach the Word of God to their children (Deuteronomy 6:4–9; Ephesians 6:4).

Volume 5 April 2023 Southwestern D6 Family Ministry Journal

Contents

Practitioner Insights

Book Reviews

Editorial

We are confronted with the reality that the next generation in our churches live in a secular world, daily navigating a culture that knows nothing of Christ, His values, or His Word. The sweeping current of the cultural streams prove strong, often pulling children, youth, and families further and further away from God's truth. Family ministry, therefore, responds, in part, by equipping this generation to biblically engage the culture around them and by cultivating a biblical worldview in the hearts of young people today. This is an urgent, critical, challenging, life-long ministry for both the church and the home. It is also a joyful calling shared by church leaders and parents.

The *Southwestern D6 Family Ministry Journal Volume 5* is a unique edition as half of our articles emphasize the theme of Equipping the Next Generation With a Biblical Worldview. The papers focused on this theme include a variety of approaches. Allen Jackson's article examines the challenges of discipleship in a post-truth culture and contrasts this with Jesus' words of truth, which prove to be much more than just a concept or worldview. Paul Mermilliod provides a synthesis of a quantitative analysis study as he draws implications for today's church focused on equipping families with a biblical worldview. June Lee's research emphasizes the role of spiritual disciplines when building a biblical worldview for children. Each of these offer insight and application for both families and church families. One of our practitioner insights, written by Travis Flanagan, also confronts competing worldviews, contrasting cultural and biblical views of marriage and family.

Rebecca Aniol, Eddy Wu, and Gady Youmans explore other aspects of passing down faith and cultivating worldview. Aniol's article contends that educational textbooks and curriculum must go further than simply presenting true information and must engage the heart through living language. Wu focuses specifically on resources that prepare teenagers to respond to the problem of evil philosophically, emotionally, and intellectually. In yet another practitioner insight, Youmans shares testimony of a program in partnership with Georgia public schools that allows teenagers to attend Bible classes daily, further shaping a biblical worldview.

Outside of this theme, Volume 5 of our journal includes several other articles. Matthew McCraney's research presents both obstacles and opportunities for churches to better partner with parents of special needs children in order to love and disciple these children. Thomas Bergler argues that recent research reveals that Christian parents see themselves as responsible for the discipleship of their children and, therefore, Bergler issues a call for reframing family ministry in light of this insight. Bergler's analysis is complimented by Graham Hale's review of the biblical commands for family discipleship.

Chris Shirley and I teamed up together to develop a practical theology of the Gospel's impact on the home. Our paper recognizes a family framework woven together with the Gospel throughout the Old and New Testaments, reminding us of the power of the Gospel to transform families still today. Rich Griffith offers our third practitioner insight, presenting more than a dozen ways parents can disciple their children daily. Finally, Gareth Crispin uses research from three churches in England to weigh the relationship between theology and family ministry. His study invites church leaders to consider the effect their theological positions have on their ministry to families.

As our journal continues to put forth research, essays, articles, insights, and reviews that champion generational discipleship as seen in Deuteronomy 6, our team is privileged to present our fifth volume. With ten academic articles, three practitioner insights, and seven book reviews, the pages to follow include both scholarly research for the academic community and biblical encouragement for those serving in the local church and other parachurch ministries. These submissions engage varying aspects of family ministry, family needs, generational discipleship, youth ministry, children's ministry, culture, education, and practical theology.

I am thankful for the expertise of our writers and for the time they devoted to their papers. Most importantly, however, I am thankful for the hearts of these leaders and their passion for family ministry and generational discipleship. I believe that each work presented is beneficial for the academy, the church, and the home. Our prayer is that your readings here will further encourage your ministry there so that the next generation will stand firm in the midst of cultural streams and set their hope in God alone (Psalm 78:7).

Jonathan Williams, Ph.D.
Managing Editor, *Southwestern D6 Family Ministry Journal*

Reframing Family Ministry in Light of How Christian Parents Really Think

Thomas E. Bergler, Ph.D.

Abstract: Family ministry advocates claim that Christian parents are abdicating their responsibility and that restructuring church life to re-engage parents will build lasting faith in children. Recent research on religious parenting shows that Christian parents already see themselves as primarily responsible and do not look to their congregations for help as much as they should. Meanwhile, the firmly and nearly universally held cultural beliefs that shape how Christian parents approach the task of passing on their faith only partially support biblical discipleship. In order to achieve its goals, the family ministry movement must devise strategies to address these cultural beliefs.

Reframing Family Ministry in Light of How Christian Parents Really Think

Family ministry advocates within Conservative Protestant circles commonly assert that Christian parents are abdicating their responsibility as the primary disciplers of their children, that youth ministries and other age-specific ministry models are to blame for this parental neglect, and that these factors account for an increasing number of young adults leaving the church. The solution to these problems, they say, is to restructure church life to reflect a family ministry strategy designed to equip parents for their discipling role. In light of recent research on religious parenting, family ministry proponents need to revise both their understanding of the challenges they face and at least some of their proposed solutions.

This new research shows that Christian parents see themselves, not their congregations, as primarily responsible for passing on the faith to their children. These same parents hold firmly to a nearly universal set of American cultural beliefs about intergenerational faith transmission. Unfortunately, some of these convictions are likely to hinder the process of forming life-long disciples of Jesus in partnership with the church. These foundational beliefs about parenting are sustained by significant long-term changes in the place of religion in American life and in modern western conceptions of the self. Family ministry must be reframed in light of how Christian parents really think about their task and why they think that way.

How Family Ministry Advocates Frame Their Task

There are two main groups of writers focusing on intergenerational faith transmission in the conservative Protestant world. One group uses the phrase "family ministry," to describe their project while another group uses phrases like "intergenerational ministry" or "intergenerational Christian formation" (Allen & Santos, 2020; Kjesbo & Cha, 2020; Mermilliod, 2020). Both groups assert that churches should significantly revise their strategies and practices to enable intergenerational faith transmission. Both groups ground their projects in biblical theologies of family, church, and faith formation. Both groups identify age segregation in churches as one cause of poor faith formation outcomes. Where the two groups differ is in their proposed solutions. Intergenerational ministry advocates prioritize church-based environments in which believers of all ages who are not necessarily biologically related to each other engage in faith formation activities together (Allen, 2018; Allen & Ross, 2012; Allen & Santos, 2020). Family ministry strategists argue for the God-given central role of parents and so their strategies rely more heavily on parental motivation and competence. Both groups can benefit from the analysis of how religious parents think about their task as described in this article, but family ministry leaders have even more at stake since by their own standards, their projects are not successful unless parents are engaged in quality faith formation with their children at home. For these reasons, this article will be primarily addressed to those who describe their work as "family ministry."

Many of the leaders of the family ministry movement were drawn to the topic by concern about the young adults they saw leaving the church after high school graduation. They were also frustrated with the level of youth discipleship and parental engagement they were able to achieve through the ministry models they had learned in seminary. They began to wonder if these were systemic problems that required new strategies and structures for youth discipleship. These personal ministry experiences shaped how they framed the challenges and opportunities of family ministry (Hunter, 2015; Joiner, 2009; Jones, ed. 2009; Shirley, 2018; Walker 2013).

Why were too many young people leaving the church? Because parents were not shouldering their God-given responsibility to form their children in the faith. For example, Timothy Paul Jones wrote that "thousands of hours" of research have convinced him that "The overwhelming majority of Christian parents are not actively engaged in any sort of battle for their children's souls." (Jones, 2011, p. 25). Why aren't parents more involved? The most common answer to that question among family ministry writers is that age segregated, specialized programs in churches encourage parents to delegate the spiritual formation of their offspring to the religious professionals (Hunter, 2015; Jones, 2011). Still, family ministry authors believe that Christian parents usually want to contribute to the spiritual growth of their children, but don't know how (Hunter 2015; Joiner, 2009; Jones, 2011). Family ministry leaders frame their challenge as "How can we motivate and equip parents to assume their God-given responsibility as the primary disciplers of their children?" The solutions proposed typically involve some combination of training parents for their role, implementing a church-wide family ministry strategy that eliminates or significantly restructures age specific ministries, and creating curriculum materials that facilitate intergenerational faith conversations and rites of passage (Hunter, 2015; Joiner, 2009; Jones, ed. 2009; Kjesbo & Cha, 2020; Mermilliod, 2020; Shirley, 2018; Walker 2013).

Family ministry authors are well aware of a wide range of negative influences on Christian parents and children in the wider culture (Anthony & Anthony, 2011; Shirley, 2018; Stinson & Jones, 2011). What has been missing until now was detailed information about the ways that cultural values are shaping the thinking of even the most religious parents in America. As it turns out, even the parents who are most committed to the faith and the church hold beliefs about faith transmission that may hinder family ministry efforts.

How Christian Parents Really Think About Passing on the Faith

How do religious parents think about their task of transmitting faith to their children? In *Religious Parenting: Transmitting Faith and Values in Contemporary America* (2020), Smith, Ritz, and Rotolo report their answer to that question. They conducted 235 in depth interviews with a wide variety of the more religious parents in America. Although they did not have a nationally representative sample, the researchers did not see this as a significant problem because they wanted to know what the more religious parents in America think. And since so little previous research had investigated this topic, they felt justified in providing a solid beginning.

To their surprise, Smith et al. found that their interview subjects all spoke in the same ways about their task. Although there are many differences between, for example, a white conservative Protestant and a Thai immigrant Buddhist, when asked about their beliefs regarding the meaning of life, how the world works, their hopes for their children and for their family life, and how all of that applies to their religious parenting strategies, their answers were very similar. It was as if the parents in the study had been indoctrinated in a particular way of thinking about religious parenting. Some minor variations based on differences in their religious traditions did appear in the interviews, but these differences were rare and usually involved matters that the parents themselves regarded as secondary. The authors summarized what they call the "cultural model" of intergenerational religious transmission this way:

> Parents are responsible for preparing their children for the challenging journey of life, during which they will hopefully become their best possible selves and live happy, good lives. Religion provides crucial help for navigating life's journey successfully, including moral guidance, emotional support, and a secure home base. So, parents should equip their children with knowledge of their religion by routinely modeling its practices, values, and ethics, which children will then hopefully absorb

and embrace for themselves (Smith, Ritz, & Rotolo, 2020, p. 10–11).

The authors exhaustively documented each phrase in this summary with numerous direct quotes from their interviews. They included this extensive documentation because they anticipated skepticism about the uniformity of belief, they found among such a religiously and ethnically diverse sample of parents. And this surprisingly high degree of uniformity also suggests that while there may be some pockets of religious parents in America who do not fit the mold, most have probably been significantly formed by these cultural beliefs about religious parenting. The more religious parents in America really do share a set of foundational beliefs about their task.

The authors further analyzed their interview transcripts to find ten additional "cultural models" that support the way parents think about intergenerational faith transmission. These cultural models are: "Life's Purpose," "Life in the World," "Religion's Value," "Religious Truth," "The Nature of Children," "The Task of Parenting," "The Importance of Family Solidarity," "Why Parents Should Pass Religion on to Children," "The Role of Religious Congregations," and "How to Pass Religion to Children" (Smith, Ritz, & Rotolo, 2020). The authors carefully documented each claim about what parents believe with numerous direct quotes from their interviews. Family ministry leaders would do well to read the 250-word summaries of what parents in the study believed regarding each of these ten topics. The easiest way to access these summaries is to read chapter one of the second book that came from this study, *Handing Down the Faith* (Smith & Adamczyk, 2021).

Many of the beliefs that religious parents hold are compatible with family ministry goals and strategies. Parents believe they are responsible for raising their children in the faith. They see religion as a good thing and appreciate help from their congregations in teaching the content of the faith to their children. They want their children to live good lives: happy, moral, helping others. They see religion as a resource for helping their children stay on the right path in life, overcome challenges, and become their best selves. They value religion as a source of family solidarity and hope their children will share the parents' faith throughout their lives. Parents know they must model the faith for their children and want to avoid alienating them or provoking them to rebellion by being too heavy handed about religion (Smith, Ritz, & Rotolo, 2020; Smith & Adamczyk, 2021). All of these elements of the American cultural model of religious parenting suggest that Christian parents will be amenable to the theologies and strategies proposed by family ministry leaders.

Yet there is also reason for concern in what religious parents believe about parenting. First, Christian parenting does not seem to be very theological. The parents in the study did not talk much about conversion, salvation, the afterlife, or any specific theological beliefs or distinctive elements of their faith tradition. Even Conservative Protestants, who tended to talk a bit more about such matters in the interviews, focused on the benefits of Christian faith for their children's lives in this world, not on eternity (Smith, Ritz, & Rotolo, p. 27). In contrast, all religious parents talked a lot about transmitting their "values" to their children:

> Parents almost never spelled out the specific content of their values. But the idea suggested general concerns, standards, and principles that parents deemed vital to hold. Parents thought it absolutely crucial to pass on their values to their children, who they sincerely hoped would embrace and share them. Very rarely did parents speak as insistently about passing on the particular cultures, discourses, and rituals of their religious traditions. Religion actually seemed to comprise a subset of their larger body of values. Indeed, it was common for parents to say that they would not mind too much if their children switched to a somewhat different religion or married someone of a dissimilar religion, as long as they all still shared the same "values." (Smith, Ritz, & Rotolo, 2020, p. 270).

This emphasis on religion as a source of "values" was one of the most common beliefs expressed in the interviews, and "nobody ever doubted, questioned, or contradicted it." Even more, as they talked about the value of religion, parents communicated the underlying idea that "helping people 'be good' essentially defines what religion *is*, what religion's basic purpose in life is about" (Smith & Adamczyk, 2021, p. 18).

On the positive side, parents in the study see religion as "a normal, valuable, meaningful, and worthy part of life, at least in its general principles" and not to be treated with "skepticism or indifference." In addition to helping people have good values and see the "big picture" of life, parents value religion for providing feelings of "peace, comfort, protection, and belonging" (Smith & Adamczyk, 2021, p. 18). They also see religion as valuable because it promotes good citizenship, strengthens society, and provides family cohesion. Finally, it keeps people on the right path in life, since we all tend to stray. There was little mention of the gospel or the need for salvation in the interviews.

Parents articulated an instrumental and therapeutic view of religion and religious truths (Smith, Ritz, & Rotolo, 2020, p. 265). They think it is important that their children learn to "believe in something," that is, that "there is a greater picture" such as "a God who is with us and answers prayers." Children must also learn that "religion can help people live good lives in this world." Beyond these basic insights, parents believe that "one can take from one's own religious tradition the parts that make sense and work best and leave the parts that don't" because "nobody needs to accept or be subject to the whole package of a religious tradition" (Smith & Adamczyk, 2021, p. 20, 22). Some parents did talk about matters related to salvation and the afterlife, or about the importance of prayer, the Bible, or other distinctive religious practices or doctrines, but these items did not constitute the heart of what parents hope to convey. That is probably because "For few American parents does religion singularly determine their understanding of the ultimate purpose and expected experience of life" (Smith and Adamczyk, 2021, p. 17). If parents see their faith as having inherent value, as being an "end in itself," they did not say so in the interviews.

Many Christian parents do not prioritize creating lifelong disciples of Jesus who are devoted to countercultural kingdom living. Rather, they see religion as a resource to help their children become their "best selves" and navigate the challenges of life. Parents also think that sharing religious beliefs and practices can create family closeness, which is one reason they hope their children will stay in the same religious tradition. On the other hand, if other activities, such as youth sports, seem to produce family togetherness at the expense of going to church, many Christian parents are not too concerned (Smith & Adamczyk, 2021, p. 28). Thus, for many religiously committed parents, religion is functioning as one resource among many in what some researchers have called the "intensive" or "concerted cultivation" parenting style. In this parenting style, parents expend considerable time, energy, and money in curating life experiences for their children designed to help them become "successful" and "happy" in such a way that they can compete effectively for their share of limited economic and educational opportunities. Intensive parenting has become normative in the minds of American parents across the spectrum of economic and racial diversity (Pinsker, 2019). In this parenting style, the focus is on the child's future prospects, and resources like churches, sports, and other extracurricular activities serve as somewhat interchangeable means toward that end.

Meanwhile, parents' biggest fears are that their children take the wrong path in life, including rebelling against the faith. Parents tend to undersell their faith, focusing on setting an example and waiting for opportunities to talk about faith rather than initiating such conversations (Smith, Ritz, & Rotolo, 2020, p. 274–275). Even parents who make faith transmission their highest parenting priority find themselves in what Smith and his research team call the "force/choice" dilemma (Smith, Ritz, & Rotolo, 2020, p. 274). Parents are well aware that they need to intentionally steer their children toward the faith, yet they see faith as a personal choice that the child must make. Parents worry that pushing too hard will have a negative effect.

This reluctance to push too hard creates a gap between how parents think about faith transmission and the actual practices that have been proven effective. Several important research studies have shown that parents who rate religion as of high importance to them personally, attend church, serve in church, engage in personal spiritual disciplines, and talk regularly with their children about faith are more likely to produce offspring who are strong in faith as young adults (Smith & Snell, 2009; Smith & Adamczyk, 2021). The parents interviewed by Smith et al. did not seem aware of the importance of frequent faith conversations for faith transmission. Instead, they believed that if the modeling process worked right, "children will over time learn, absorb, and embrace their own version of that faith, almost unconsciously" (Smith & Adamczyk, 2021, p. 33).

Crucial Trends for Intergenerational Religious Transmission

In *Handing Down the Faith*, Smith and Adamczyk summarized factors that have been shown by multiple research studies to be effective in intergenerational religious transmission, with family relationships and faith conversations being especially important. Effective parents have "warm, affirming relations" with their children that are expressed in faith conversations. These conversations involve children asking questions about faith that relate to their daily lives, with parents doing a lot of listening. Parents try to help the children understand their faith's beliefs and practices. Family conversations about faith are "not rigid or highly controlled." When parents "talk too much, make demands without explanations, force unwanted conversations, and restrict discussions to topics that they control" then faith conversations are likely to be "ineffective or counterproductive." Overall, "too much or too little religious socialization" can cause problems (Smith & Adamczyk, 2021, p. 5–6). The most effective type of faith conversation for long term faith transmission "unaffectedly flows in and out of larger discussions" rather than beginning with, "Okay, children, now we are going to talk about religion" (Smith & Adamczyk, 2021, p. 84). Such conversations also have the benefit of teaching children the everyday relevance of religion to all areas of life. Parents who are "intentional, consistent, and actively engaged but neither hands-off nor overbearing" seem to be the most effective. The role of fathers seems to be especially important, with the father's involvement and example being especially influential on children. Research also shows that two-parent households in which both parents share the same faith tradition and families in which grandparents contribute positively to faith formation also find more success in intergenerational faith formation (Smith & Adamczyk, 2021, p. 5–6).

This list of factors can be interpreted to confirm parents' fear of being too heavy handed with faith conversations. But it seems that parents have over-reacted in the opposite direction. The parents' "cultural models" of religious transmission speak almost exclusively of modeling the faith. Smith and Adamczyk (2021) made use of the longitudinal data from the National Study of Youth and Religion to analyze how religious parenting impacts children. Confirming previous studies, they found that parental religiosity is the single most important predictor of faith outcomes in children. In addition, "authoritative parenting," in which both parental expectations and parent-child emotional closeness are high, has an independent effect in predicting stronger religion in young adult children compared to other parenting styles. Parents who are highly religious get an extra "boost" from the authoritative parenting style (Smith & Adamczyk, 2021, p. 218). Parents who have daily or weekly conversations with their children about faith significantly reduce the risk that their children will never attend religious services as young adults. In fact, this new research showed that parents talking regularly with their children about faith is even more strongly associated with higher child religiosity ten years later than parents' professed importance of faith or frequency of parental church attendance (Smith & Adamczyk, 2021, p. 53–54). The authors recommended that parents talk about faith with their children more often in everyday life, recognizing that in contemporary society, the language of faith is a foreign language that requires practice (Smith & Adamczyk, 2021, p. 71). Based on the interviews with parents, we can hypothesize that either parents do not know the "foreign language" of faith or are reluctant to practice speaking it with their children. Or perhaps they think they are talking enough with their children already. At the very least we can say the most religious parents in America do not value intentional, frequent faith conversations with their children as highly as they should.

How Christian Parents Really Think About Partnering With the Church

Parents do not seem to be ready to partner with congregations in faith transmission in the ways that many family ministry advocates might hope. Parents believe that "congregations should reinforce what parents teach at home, not determine it." Parents appreciate congregations that provide an "inviting, comfortable community and some positive experiences for children" (Smith & Adamczyk, 2020, p. 31). If kids like going to church, that makes the parents' job easier. Parents do appreciate it when churches provide some basic instruction in the faith, especially basic morality like the Ten Commandments. But overall, parents do not see their congregations as important sources of religious input that play a significant role in the lives of their children. In particular, the researchers listened in vain for parents to express any appreciation for the more "religious" elements of their congregations such as "theology, liturgy, doctrinal teachings" (Smith and Adamczyk, 2021, p. 31–32). And because they do not expect much, some parents make low investments in their congregations (Smith, Ritz, & Rotolo, 2020, p. 268). Further, parents do not see themselves as representing or advocating on behalf of their religious tradition to their children. Nor do they see themselves as "engaged in a larger collective task of transmitting their particular religious tradition from generation to generation for the sake of the life of the tradition itself." (Smith, Ritz, & Rotolo, 2020, p. 269). In their minds, faith and church are valuable to the extent that they serve their project of helping their children live good lives.

Parents' sense of personal responsibility in religious parenting is a two-edged sword. On the one hand, parents do seem to see themselves, not their churches, as responsible for passing on the faith to their children. Therefore, family ministry leaders may not need to expend as much effort as they once thought to convince parents to take responsibility. On the other hand, parents may be overconfident and ill-informed about what it takes to raise their children in the faith. And some of their default assumptions about faith transmission run counter to biblical teaching in many areas, chief among them being the purpose of life, the nature of discipleship, and the place of the church in God's plan of salvation.

Why Christian Parents Think About Passing on the Faith the Way They Do

What creates these cultural beliefs about parenting and what causes parents to be the most important players in religious socialization? In chapter three of *Handing Down the Faith*, the authors theorize that the role of religion in American society has shifted from "communal solidarity project" to "personal identity accessory" (Smith & Adamczyk, 2021, p. 73). For most Americans today, the purpose of religion is no longer to form a community of people with shared beliefs, practices, and morals. Meanwhile, what Americans expect their families to be has shifted over time from "community *social institution* to home-based *companionate relations* and then to individual *lifestyle options*" (Smith & Adamczyk, 2021, p. 76). In other words, Americans do not tend to think of families as serving some larger purpose in society (or in the kingdom of God) but rather providing private space in which individuals can experience relational closeness and develop their individual identities and potentials.

In addition, western cultures have coded religion as a personal, private matter, so people naturally assume that the home will be the primary location of religious socialization and parents should be the primary agents in that process. Smith and Adamczyk noted that their model for explaining the shifting place of religion in American society and its impact on parenting finds parallels in a dozen or more similar models created by prominent sociologists over the past sixty years who were trying to explain similar phenomena (Smith & Adamczyk, 2021, p. 79). Thus, when the authors theorized that religion now functions as a "personal identity accessory" they are on well-populated theoretical ground. The social-structural locations of congregations and families in American society really do push religious institutions into an instrumental, secondary role in people's lives.

The Impact of the Self-Reflexive Imperative on Christian Parents

In particular, Smith and Rotolo draw on the work of Margaret Archer and Anthony Giddens regarding the nature of modern selves to identify something they call the "self-reflexive imperative." In modern western societies, the individual cannot avoid "making oneself the object of conscious scrutiny and evaluation, asking questions like, 'How am I doing? What do I care about? Am I being my true self? Why am I feeling this way? Should I be making different choices? Is there something important that I'm missing?'" (Smith & Adamczyk, 2021, p. 85). Self-reflexivity is an adaptive response to the structures of modern life that demand that the individual engage in an intensive and probably life-long self-development and self-monitoring project. There are simply fewer normative external inputs to identity and morality, and contemporary western people are wary of such "outside" influences anyway. Self-reflexivity can become self-centered, but it just as easily degenerates into "self-judging and berating" (Smith & Adamczyk, 2021, p. 86). Functionally, self-reflexivity may serve "as a key mediating mechanism between people's social structural contexts and their personal, ultimate concerns and actions" (Smith & Adamczyk, 2021, p. 86). In other words, developing skills for self-reflexivity is necessary for being able to reconcile external demands with one's internal sense of self without going off the rails in one direction or another. What all this means for parenting is that parents instinctively realize that their children are ultimately in the driver's seat about what kinds of people they will become and about whether Christian faith is "who they are." Parents are trying their best to help their children learn to become healthy, Christian, self-reflexive individuals, but this is a tricky business with many pitfalls and wrong turns, and parents are keenly aware of the limits of their influence.

The Impact of Expressive Individualism on Christian Parents

Why do contemporary Americans believe they should use their faith as an "identity accessory" in the particular ways that they do? Specifically with regard to family ministry, why are religious parents so united in how they think about the proper role of religion in their children's lives? Here recent work by Carl R. Trueman in *The Rise and Triumph of the Modern Self* proves helpful. Trueman set out to investigate how it has come to be that when someone says, "I am a woman trapped in a man's body," many people in western societies will not only regard this as a statement that makes sense but will suspect that anyone who questions it is immoral or stupid (Trueman, 2020, p. 19). Trueman compellingly argued that what we call the sexual revolution is really a symptom of a more fundamental revolution in our shared conceptions of the self. Drawing on the works of Charles Taylor, Philip Rieff, and Alistair McIntyre, Trueman reconstructed the historical changes that have resulted in what Taylor called "expressive individualism" and Rieff called the "psychological self." Taylor and Rieff share the conviction that modern people hold to a sense of personhood that "has almost completely dispensed with the idea of any authority beyond that of personal, psychological conviction" (Trueman, 2020, p. 36). Modern selves do not see the world as having inherent meaning, order, and purpose which they must find and to which they must conform. Rather, the world is "raw material out of which meaning and purpose can be crafted by the individual" (Trueman, 2020, p. 39). Modern selves look to discover their sense of identity not by conforming to what is taught by society and its institutions, but through the "inward quest for personal psychological happiness" (Trueman, 2020, p. 45).

Community norms and institutions are only good when they protect and support individuals in finding and expressing their identities: "Outward institutions become in effect the servants of the individual and her inner sense of well-being" (Trueman, 2020, p. 48). It is difficult for modern people to value being formed by their religious communities because, "Institutions cease to be places for the formation of individuals via their schooling in the various practices and disciplines that allow them to take their place in society. Instead, they become platforms for performance, where individuals are allowed to become their authentic selves precisely because they are able to give expression to who they are 'inside'" (Trueman, 2020, p. 49).

The beliefs parents hold about passing on the faith to their children are just the kinds of beliefs we would expect in a society characterized by the "self-reflexive imperative," "expressive individualism," and the "psychological self." Religious parents believe that each child "possesses within themselves a 'best self they can be,' something like an inherent, unique, and inalienable ideal personality and optimal life-to-be-lived" (Smith & Adamczyk, 2021, p. 24). This "best self" is an "inherent potential" that must be cultivated especially in the "first half of life." To be successful, children need to overcome the problems and trials that come in life and as they do, they will experience "positive growth, maturity, and understanding." The alternative is for children to "become compromised or wrecked by the inability to overcome the hardships" of life and so "fail to realize the 'best selves' they could have been" (Smith & Adamczyk, 2021, p. 24).

Parents see life as a "journey" and religion learned at home as a "home base" or "grounding" from which to launch that journey. These two clusters of metaphors (foundation and journey) were among the most common in the interviews, with a full 100% of the interviewees using some kind of "journey" metaphor (Smith, Ritz, & Rotolo, 2020, p. 37). Parents are well aware that "the culture sends some 'bad messages'" that must be recognized and resisted. They realize that each child will face trials, mistakes, and discouragement, but the job of a good parent is to equip the child with resources to overcome such challenges. Only children who have "a solid internal 'grounding,' a 'true sense of self,'" will navigate the journey of life successfully (Smith & Adamczyk, 2021, p. 16).

Parents hope to steer their children toward the "good life" which is one in which "self-directed individuals are happy, live ethically, work hard, enjoy family and friends, and help other people." But the good life is not primarily an external standard to which Christians must conform, rather "Good lives must be self-determined and pursued in ways that are true to each unique individual self." To be fair, Christian parents do not want their children to be "individual*istic* in the sense of isolated or selfish." Parents believe they need to equip their children for "the task of self-realization," yet "each individual must find his or her own particular way to discover their own purpose and lead a good life true to who they are as a unique self" (Smith & Adamczyk, 2021, 14). When religious parents speak of the "journey" of life, what they mean is not "stay on this trail" but rather "you must find your own path," at least once you grow up (Smith & Adamczyk, p. 15).

It is easy to see how "expressive individualism" and the resulting "cultural models" of religious parenting can undermine life-long discipleship and loyalty to the church. First, faith is easily called into question or discarded if the individual perceives that it is not living up to its job of helping navigate the challenging journey of life. And faith is primarily important in the first half of life, giving young people a "home base." Further, faith is individualized, and communities of faith are optional lifestyle enhancements. If faith is a personal life enhancer, then it is not hard to see how doctrine and theology could be seen as of secondary importance. Only "values" and the "big picture" of the faith matter. Family ministry advocates who attempt to make the nuclear family the center of faith formation may be unintentionally reinforcing the cultural belief that congregations and the faith traditions they represent are of only secondary, instrumental value. Even parents and families, it must be noted, are envisioned in this set of beliefs as an optional "home base." It is really the child's independent, happy, "good person" future which is the focus of adult attention in the church and the home.

Reframing Family Ministry

Up to now, family ministry leaders have framed their challenge as a systemic failure of faith formation resulting in too few young people who are raised in church becoming life-long followers of Jesus. The causes of this problem have been identified as parents not shouldering their responsibility as primary disciplers of their children and the church enabling that abdication through ill-conceived, age-graded ministries. Proposed solutions have included restructuring or even eliminating age-specific ministries and equipping parents with resources for conducting faith formation activities at home. In light of how Christian parents really think about their task, this way of framing family ministry could easily be overwhelmed by the powerful cultural beliefs that shape religious parenting in America. Smith et al. put it this way: "Any distinctive teachings of American religious traditions about passing on faith and practice to children is overshadowed and overwhelmed by the governing power of the dominant models and metaphors shared by most religious parents across all traditions" (Smith, Ritz, & Rotolo, 2020, p. 272–273). As a result, even highly involved Christian parents may be primarily interested in forming their children into "good people" with "good values" who can navigate the "journey of life" and become their "best selves." These "good people" may not have experienced conversion, may know little theology, and may have little loyalty to their congregations or faith traditions. They may well regard the church, the faith, and even God himself as optional, temporary lifestyle enhancements whose primary purpose is helping them discover and express their self-defined identity. But "good people" like that are not the disciples of Jesus that family ministry leaders hope the parents in their churches will raise. So, the family ministry project, as currently framed, may fail on its own terms unless it develops strategies to counter the "cultural models of religious parenting."

How should family ministry be reframed? First, focus should shift from convincing parents to take responsibility for faith formation of their children toward re-training parents in a biblical vision for parenting. In particular, family ministry leaders need to read chapter one of *Handing Down the Faith* and conduct a point-by-point theological analysis of the "cultural models of religious parenting" found there. Then leaders need to develop teachings and practices which re-form parents away from the "cultural models" and toward a Christian theological vision for parenting.

Many Christian parents will be cooperative with this process of re-training. Smith, Ritz, and Rotolo remind us that, "Most of the parents we interviewed turned out to be serious, caring, thoughtful people trying their best to raise their kids in often difficult situations and in a culture they experience as seriously problematic" (2020, p. 273). The researchers further noted that one reason for the nearly universal appeal of the "cultural models of religious parenting" is that they "make logical, coherent sense" to parents even if they are not the same set of beliefs that religious leaders might choose (2020, p. 273). Family ministry leaders need to carefully examine the appeal and coherence of these common beliefs about parenting and if possible, create an equally coherent body of Christian teaching on parenting. Christian parents really do want their children to become life-long followers of Jesus, but they need more and better teaching on the biblical goals of Christian parenting, with clear explanations of how those goals contrast with the goals found in the "cultural models" of religious parenting. In particular, teaching about the image of God, identity in Christ, the mission of the church, and the communal dimensions of Christianity are both urgently needed and highly susceptible to misinterpretation by Christians formed in the current cultural milieu. Parents need to be gently shown how some of their own assumptions about parenting may be undermining their stated goals of long-term faith commitment and church involvement on the part of their children.

Second, family ministry leaders need to partner with parents to encourage children toward an experiential relationship with Jesus through the Holy Spirit. For some reason, the Christian parents interviewed by Smith et al. did not see conversion or other religious experiences as important in the faith formation of their children. Yet research has shown that religious experiences during adolescence are an important factor predicting stronger young adult faith (Smith & Snell, 2009). The days in which childhood or teenage conversions were at times overemphasized or in which parents felt pressure to lead their children in the sinner's prayer seem to be waning if not long gone. More common today might be missed opportunities to help young people make a decision to follow Christ or to learn how to have ongoing experiences of God.

Third, family ministry leaders need to provide even more guidance and support to parents as they navigate the "force/choice dilemma." Parents experience a lot of doubt, fear, and uncertainty as they try to influence their children to embrace the faith without alienating them. "Conservative Protestant parents tend simultaneously to be highly invested in their children remaining 'in the faith' *and* to view faith as needing to be an authentic, individual, personal choice, resulting in the force/choice dilemma impinging on these parents with particular force" (Smith, Ritz, & Rotolo, 2020, p. 274–276). Too many parents wrongly assume that modeling the faith and only rarely talking about it will be enough. We now know what kinds of parent-child faith conversations are most likely to contribute to lasting faith, and parents should be coached to have those kinds of conversations. As noted above, these conversations should be frequent, flow-ing from everyday activities and concerns, and involve much listening and warmth from parents (Smith & Adamczyk, p. 5, 53–54). Family ministry leaders should consider learning more about the "authoritative parenting" style and incorporating those insights into parenting seminars so that families will be more likely to have the kinds of relationships that allow fruitful faith conversations. Christian parents will be eager to receive any credible, compassionate help the church can provide as they face what they consider to be one of their most difficult challenges.

Fourth, church leaders should evaluate and modify their ministry structures and strategies in light of the "cultural models of religious parenting." It seems obvious that in the biblical witness, both Israel and the Church are portrayed more like "communal solidarity projects" than "personal identity accessories." Are members of our congregations learning to view the Church as God's people who are being formed by him in a shared way of life and mission? What specific strategies, structures, relationships, and practices do we have in place to steer church members toward a biblical vision of the Christian life, the church, and the mission of God? Which existing strategies, structures, or practices need to be reformed or replaced?

One specific recommendation in this regard is for family ministry leaders to incorporate even more church-based, dialogical, intergenerational faith formation activities into their overall strategies. Good curriculum materials for use at home can help, but it is likely that even theologically and pedagogically sound materials could be diluted by the cultural models of religious parenting. Those parents most formed by the patterns of thought discovered by Smith et al. will probably need to see intergenerational faith activities modeled, then try them with others at church, and finally try to lead them at home on their own. Here the "family ministry" movement could fruitfully collaborate with and learn from the "intergenerational ministry" movement. Intergenerational faith formation at church may also take some of the pressure off parents with regard to the force/choice dilemma. The current default assumption is that family and church exist to serve the individualized development of the self. Both parents and children need to experience a different reality in which God forms his family, the church, as the context in which family units and their members can find their true identities and purposes. If when the church gathers, its teachings, worship, and other practices display the inherent value of the whole family of God and promote dialogical identity formation, that will provide a much healthier context for disciples of all ages to grow to maturity in Christ.

References

Allen, H. C., ed. (2018). *Intergenerate: Transforming churches through intergenerational ministry.* Abilene, TX: Abilene Christian University Press.

Allen, H. C. and Ross, C. L. (2012). *Intergenerational Christian formation: Bringing the whole church together in ministry, community and worship.* Downers Grove, IL: IVP Academic.

Allen, H. C. and Santos, J. B. (2020). Intergenerational ministry—a forty-year perspective: 1980–2020. *Christian Education Journal* 17(3): 506–529.

Anthony, M. and Anthony, M. (2011). *A theology for family ministries.* Nashville, TN: B & H Publishing Group.

Hunter, R. (2015). *The DNA of D6: Building blocks of generational discipleship.* Nashville, TN: Randall House.

Joiner, R. (2009). *Think orange: Imagine the impact when church and family collide.* Colorado Springs, CO: David C. Cook Publishing.

Jones, T. P. (2011). *Family ministry field guide: How your church can equip parents to make disciples.* Indianapolis, IN: Wesleyan Publishing House.

Jones, T. P., ed. (2009). *Perspectives on family ministry: 3 Views.* Nashville, TN: B & H Academic.

Kjesbo, D. M. and Cha, L. Y. (2020). Family ministry: Past, present, future. *Christian Education Journal* 17(3): 488–505.

Mermilliod, E. P. (2020). A synthesis of academic research related to church-based family ministry. *Christian Education Journal.* DOI 10.1177/0739891320974383

Pinsker, J. (2019). 'Intensive' parenting is now the norm in America. *The Atlantic* (Jan. 16, 2019) retrieved from https://www.theatlantic.com/family/archive/2019/01/intensive-helicopter-parenting-inequality/580528/ on 9/29/2021

Shirley, C. (2018). *Family ministry and the church: A leader's guide for ministry through families.* Nashville, TN: Randall House.

Smith, C. and Adamczyk, A. (2021). *Handing down the faith: How parents pass their religion on to the next generation.* New York: Oxford University Press.

Smith, C. and Denton, M. L. (2005). *Soul searching: The religious and spiritual lives of American teenagers.* New York: Oxford University Press.

Smith, C., Ritz, B. and Rotolo, M (2020). *Religious parenting: Transmitting faith and values in contemporary America.* Princeton, NJ: Princeton University Press.

Smith, C. and Snell, P. (2009). *Souls in transition: The religious and spiritual lives of emerging Adults.* New York: Oxford University Press.

Stinson, R & Jones, T., eds. (2011). *Trained in the fear of God: Family ministry in theological, historical, and practical perspective.* Grand Rapids, MI: Kregel Publications.

Walker, M. (2013). *Intergenerational youth ministry*. Vision for Youth Publishing.

Author Biography

Thomas E. Bergler, Ph.D., serves as professor of Christian Thought and Practice at Huntington University where he has taught theology, youth ministry and discipleship courses for 21 years. He is the author of *The Juvenilization of American Christianity* (William B. Eerdmans Publishing Company) and *From Here to Maturity: Overcoming the Juvenilization of American Christianity* (Williams B. Eerdmans Publishing Company).

Gospel Family: A Practical Theology of the Gospel's Impact on the Home

Chris Shirley, Ph.D., and Jonathan Williams, Ph.D.

Abstract: The Gospel message woven throughout the Scriptures proclaims the reconstitution of God's family into a Kingdom of sons and daughters who share a common Spirit and serve a common King. The Gospel is about the movement of God—from before the beginning of time to the culmination of His eternal plan—to establish a Kingdom and create a family to live and flourish in His Kingdom. The Gospel is about the fall of God's children into sin and rebellion as they rejected His authority and walked away from the protection and sufficiency of His Kingdom. The Gospel is a message of God's forgiveness for His wayward children if they would only repent, believe, and follow the One God established as supreme ruler of His Kingdom: Jesus the Son, Jesus the King. The Gospel proclaims the reconstitution of God's family into a Kingdom of sons and daughters who share a common Spirit and serve a common King. Within this Gospel framework is a message about family and relationships. This article seeks to understand the biblical and theological message of the Gospel and its transformational impact on the family and the home, granting specific focus to family worship as a means to bring the Gospel into the home today.

Introduction

"The Gospel is not a doctrine of the tongue, but of life. It cannot be grasped by reason and memory only, but it is fully understood when it possesses the whole soul and penetrates to the inner recesses of the heart."
John Calvin

There is a growing conversation among contemporary Christian scholars and authors related to the need for a concise and compelling definition of the Gospel. Snodgrass (2022) claimed that the church offers only a "deficient, inept, and inert Gospel ... that is neither compelling nor taken seriously" (pp. 3–4). Joining Snodgrass, Hull (2016) entered the conversation by claiming modern evangelicalism has reduced the Gospel to the plan of salvation alone (pp. 30–31). McKnight (2016) quoted Piper's definition of the Gospel—"justification by faith"—and questioned the Gospel being reduced to only a theological formulation (p. 25). Pointing out a need for more precision, Bates (2021) claimed that in a world in which a multitude of Gospel definitions offer only "cultural stories about how to achieve full human flourishing," the church needs to provide a precise and compelling Gospel that is biblically cogent and spiritually transforming (p. 22).

John Calvin's statement above expresses the need for a definition of the Gospel that is synergistic, where the whole is greater than the sum of its parts. The Gospel should certainly include a necessary plan of salvation. Justification-by-faith describes the point of contact between God and man that regenerates a dead spirit into a one that is living and eternal; but this is not the complete message of the Gospel. As Calvin states, the Gospel is a "doctrine ... of life ... that possesses the whole soul and penetrates ... the heart." The Gospel should be understood as the meaning and purpose of life, not just the solution to an existential problem. The Gospel is not about seeing Jesus as a utilitarian means to an end; rather, the Gospel is about seeing Jesus "as He is" (1 John 3:2) and, in doing so, becoming "like Him" (1 John 3:2).

Perhaps the Gospel is too broad to be limited to one defining statement; this may be because the Gospel is not a proposition but a person, and our relationship with that person: Jesus Christ. Snodgrass (2022) suggested the Gospel is about *participation*: "The Gospel is about God's participation with us and our participation with God." He claimed the Gospel offers us an opportunity for "being family" with God ... (p. 6). Our participation with God, as His sons and daughters, is effectuated through a relationship with His Son. In *The King Jesus Gospel*, McKnight (2016) defined the Gospel as the story of God's Son: the Messiah Jesus, His kingdom, His kingship, and His coming rule over a new creation (p. 97). More succinctly, Bates (2021) related the Gospel message in one phrase: "Jesus is the Christ" (p. 24).

Consider the following propositions. (1) The Gospel is about the movement of God—from before the beginning of time to the culmination of His eternal plan—to establish a Kingdom and create a family to live and flourish in His Kingdom. (2) The Gospel is about the fall of God's children into sin and rebellion as they rejected His authority and walked away from the protection and sufficiency of His Kingdom. (3) The Gospel is a message of God's forgiveness for His wayward children if they would only repent, believe, and follow the One God established as supreme ruler of His Kingdom: Jesus the Son, Jesus the King. (4) The Gospel proclaims the reconstitution of God's family into a Kingdom of sons and daughters who share a common Spirit and serve a common King.

God With Us: The Gospel Story of God's Family

At every point in Gospel's development, even from the beginning, God has manifested his desire to be in a familial relationship with His human creation (Shirley, 2018, p. 36): walking in the garden with Adam and Eve; dwelling with the children of Israel (Exodus 29:45); incarnated as Jesus the Messiah among His family of followers (John 1:14); dwelling in the Sprit with those who follow the Son (Romans 8:9); living forever in heavenly splendor with His bride, the saints of God in Christ (Revelation 21:3). "God with us" (Isaiah 7:14; Matthew 1:23) describes God's promise through Gospel message. He has been with us; He is with us now; and He will be with us forever.

God Was With Us: God's Family Created

Within this Gospel framework is a message about family and relationships. God was with us in the beginning when He created the world—through the work of His Son (John. 1:3–4)—and created man and woman to have a perfect and personal relationship with Him. God created the two who became one and thereby established a family. The man and woman were created in God's "image and likeness" and were commissioned to "be fruitful and multiply" His image-bearers throughout the earth (Genesis 1:26–28).

The Genesis 2 account provides qualitative insights into this pairing. God provided the gift of marriage and family as an earthly reflection of a heavenly relationship, what Chandler (2014) referred to as an "incubator of godly love and a conduit for Christian formation" (p. 108). As the two He created shared in God's relational nature, so they shared a relationship with one another. Understanding that "it is not good for the man to be alone," God created for him a "helper corresponding to him" (2:18) and brought the two together in a unique and unified relationship built on mutual faithfulness, intimacy, and commitment (Moon, 2020, p. 16). These covenant qualities are evident in the description of the first marriage in Genesis 2:21–25. Hugenberger (1997) contended the man's oath in Genesis 2:23 ("bone of my bone and flesh of my flesh") is also expressed in covenant language, validating the unity of this relationship and forming a family through the coming together of two parties in marriage (pp. 164–65). Likewise, God has invited humankind to form a covenant relationship with Himself, grounded in faithfulness, intimacy, and commitment.

However, man and woman rebelled, brought sin into the world, and destroyed the perfect and personal relationship between God and His human creation; but God promised that one day He would restore this relationship and the power of sin would be destroyed. Even in God's judgment upon the first couple, we hear whispers of the Gospel as God declares that the "offspring" of the woman would crush the head of the serpent and destroy his power over humankind (Genesis 3:15). The salvation of the fallen world would be accomplished through the family line stretching from Adam and Eve to the Messiah Jesus, who would bring peace and reconciliation between God and His fallen family.

The Gospel began its forward advance as God chose a family to carry His blessed plan into the world (Danylak, 2010, pp. 117–118). From an obscure corner of the world, God called a man named Abram, whose name means "exalted father," to establish a "great nation" of families who would bless the world (Genesis 12:2). Ironically, Abram and his wife, Sarai, were childless; yet from this barren couple God fashioned a family with one son, Isaac, who would be father of the father of God's chosen people. This father, Jacob, and his sons were the genesis of the nation of Israel, a nation composed of twelve family tribes.

Within one of these family tribes, the tribe of Judah, God chose a man named David to become king over the nation of Israel and progenitor to the One whom God would send to establish David's throne "forever" (2 Samuel 7:16). The good news of the eternal king, the Messiah, was tied to a specific family, yet His reign would affect all families on earth. Through the prophet Isaiah, God promised through the Messiah He would bring "light for the nations, that my salvation may reach to the end of the earth" (Isaiah 49:6).

Therefore, we see the Gospel from the beginning of time as a story about marriage and family (Danylak, 2020, pp. 52–53). From the point at which the woman was "taken out of man" and united with her husband, families have been a key part of God's plan to fill the world with worshippers who bring Him glory, honor, and praise. Even in their fallen state, God used families to infuse His blessing throughout the earth. These families formed into tribes, clans, and houses, becoming a nation that God called His own. Even when they rebelled and became God's prodigal children, He kept His plan intact through faithful children who maintained their faith in their one, true Father. When the fullness of time had come, God chose one family from the tribe of Judah in the line of David to deliver His greatest blessing: "Immanuel" (Isaiah 7:14), God with us, Jesus the Messiah.

God Came to Us: God's Family Reborn

The Gospel became a Person when God came to be with us in the flesh. God incarnate was born to a virgin through the power of the Holy Spirit. The Son of God, Jesus, was raised as the fully human child of Mary and her husband, Joseph; God Himself grew up in a household in Nazareth of Israel, experiencing the love and joy of family relationships as He developed in "wisdom and stature, and in favor with God and man" (Luke 2:52) as the eldest son in His family.

As Jesus grew into a man, He learned a trade in carpentry as an apprentice to his earthly father. However, when His time was ordained, Jesus left His home to serve His heavenly Father in calling humankind back into a restored relationship with their Creator: to once again be God's true sons and daughters. The beginning of Jesus' ministry occurred at His baptism when He received the blessing and stamp of approval from His Father

(Matthew 3:13–17). From that point, Jesus proclaimed that the Kingdom of God was "near" and that entrance to that Kingdom was based on repentance—turning away from sin—and obedience—turning to Jesus and following Him as His disciple (Mark 1:14–18). Jesus identified Himself as the proclaimer and embodiment of God's Gospel to the world. Through Jesus, God would bring the world back to Himself and unite God's family under His loving headship once again (John 3:16–17).

The Gospel message rose to its crescendo at the cross: the climax of the story that started in the garden. Jesus the Messiah, who came to release us from the control of sin and bring us back into God's favor in life and for eternity, willingly gave up His life as payment for our sin—"according to the Scriptures." He was resurrected from death three days later—"according to the Scriptures" (1 Corinthians 15:1–6). God offers forgiveness, restoration, and eternal life to anyone who turns from their sin, believes the truth about Jesus, and makes Him their first priority in life. One's restored relationship into God's family is actuated through faith—belief, trust, hope, allegiance—in Jesus the Christ, our co-heir in the eternal blessing God bestows on all who are in Christ (Bates, 2021, p. 93).

Bates (2017) noted that one's inculcation of Gospel allegiance or faith moves him or her into a familial relationship with the One True Father and Creator through the infusion—or indwelling—of the Spirit of God (pp. 98–99). The presence of the Spirit unites all who follow Jesus into a family of believers, which was God's intention from the beginning of time. People "from every nation, from all tribes and peoples and languages" (Revelation 7:9) become spiritual brothers and sisters alongside our co-heir and brother, Jesus Christ, in the household of God (1 Timothy 3:15). Jesus Himself described this family relationship not as a symbolic connection, but a genuine familial bond experienced by all who belong to Him (Matthew 12:46–50). Hellerman (2001) contended that siblings had the strongest and most lasting connections in the Mediterranean family model in days of the early church (pp. 35–37). Therefore, the many references in Scripture to brother-sister relationships among believers indicates the robust nature of the church as God's extended and universal family, created by the power of His Gospel and advancing the Gospel into the world.

God Will Be With Us: God's Family Restored

The family of God, as it exists on the earth in the form of the church, will one day be restored to their rightful relationship with the Lord. Scripture indicates a telos, or destiny, for God's human creation that begins with the return of Jesus Christ.

The Gospel of our eternal future remains focused on Jesus Christ and those who belong to Him. The good news is the proclamation of the returning King, who comes in victory to claim what is rightfully His. He will return to the world to accomplish for all creation what He has already accomplished in His followers; He will completely destroy sin and evil, establish a perfect Kingdom, and invite all those who love Him to be with Him forever.

The apostle Paul affirms the second coming of Christ in 1 Thessalonians 4:16–17. In Matthew 25:31–33, Jesus describes His return in majestic and triumphant terms: "When the Son of Man comes in his glory, and all the angels with him, then he will sit on his glorious throne. Before him will be gathered all the nations, and he will separate people one from another as a shepherd separates the sheep from the goats. And he will place the sheep on his right, but the goats on the left." At the end of this pericope (25:46), the king judges sin and evil by sending the unrighteous (goats) to "eternal punishment" and ushers the righteous (sheep) into "eternal life."

In the new Heaven and earth (Revelation 22:1–4), the Kingdom of God will be a reality for all those who belong to Him and are one with Him. His name will be on the "foreheads" of every citizen of this perfect Kingdom, indicating a mark of allegiance and kinship to the one true God who provides his children with "safety and protection" (Patterson, 2012, p. 377). In Revelation 21:3, the apostle John heard a loud voice from God's throne: "Behold, the dwelling place of God is with man. He will dwell with them, and they will be his people, and God himself will be with them as their God." This astounding proclamation places a bookend at the end of the Gospel story, for the purpose of God has been completed as He draws together His eternal family to be with Him in a perfect and eternal relationship of love.

The Need for the Gospel in Today's Homes

So far, we have seen that the Gospel message of God's family is one of creation, rebirth, and restoration. Just as this Gospel message is woven alongside a family framework throughout the Bible, the Gospel continues to transform families today. The remainder of this article will, therefore, examine this transformation by evaluating the need families have for the Gospel, the impact of the Gospel on families today, and the call for families to bring the Gospel into the home.

Families today remain in desperate need of the Gospel of Jesus Christ. Bryan Nelson and Timothy Paul Jones (2011) made it clear that stronger families or stronger family ministries are not the answers. "The Gospel is what changes people," they wrote, "not programs or practices; not models or methods; but solely and only the Gospel of Jesus Christ" (p. 28). Every family consists of fallen men and women in need of the Gospel. Any theology for family ministry requires a foundational affirmation of this basic truth. Just as the first family encountered sin and a promise of redemption in the same day, revealing God's promise to, "Resolve man's dilemma by pointing to a future Savior who would restore believing man to fellowship with God" (Enns, 1989, p. 42) sinful families today may encounter this promised restoration through the good news of the Gospel.

The biblical narrative and today's theology for family ministry both bloom out of this root of creation, fall, and now, a need for redemption. Wayne Grudem presented this same chronological approach, as he wrote, "The history of the human race as presented in Scripture is primarily a history of man in a state of sin and rebellion against God and of God's plan of redemption to bring man back to himself" (1994, p. 490).

This pattern of brokenness in the home and sin in the family surfaces in many homes throughout Scripture. These biblical examples bring hope to today's family searching for redemption. There are stories presented throughout the Bible that highlight the sinful state of families and the hope of redemption. From heartbreaking episodes of rape (Genesis 34) to violent chapters of murder (Genesis 4), these stories remind the reader that every family is fallen. In the book of Judges alone, "Abimelech kills seventy brothers. Jephthah is prepared to make his daughter into a sacrifice to Yahweh. A man surrenders his wife to rape and death. And the other clans determine to take action against their Benjaminite brothers, to great slaughter on both sides" (Goldingay, 2009, p. 413).

However, through this dark reality, God's Word shines a light, a thread of hope woven throughout the pages: The Gospel. Even families sitting in the rubble, grieving widows (Ruth) and adulterous husbands (David), find present restoration and a promise of a future Redeemer; a promise that still reaches families today. As Frederick Cardoza wrote, "God cares about families. He cares about nuclear families, broken families, and households of all types. He wants His timeless principles to be applied to our lives so we can see the power of the living Christ break the cycles of bondage that affect moms, dads, sons, daughters, brothers, and sisters" (2011, p. 64).

Since the greatest problem families face today remains the hopelessness of their own sin, the greatest solution available to families today remains the hope of the Gospel message that Jesus Christ came to seek and save the lost (Luke 19:10), died on the cross for our sins, was buried, and rose again on the third day (1 Corinthians 15:3–4), so that now we may be saved by grace through faith in Jesus (Ephesians 2:8). Families need this good news message. Families need all that the Gospel brings.

The Impact of the Gospel in Today's Homes

As families remain in need of the Gospel, the Gospel continues to impact hearts and homes today. The Gospel proves impactful because there is power in this good news message. Paul wrote of this power, declaring that it is "the power of God for salvation to everyone who believes" (Romans 1:16). Families that recognize their need for Christ will seek Him daily while leading their families to do the same, convinced that there is power in the Gospel to impact, save, transform, restore, and renew their home.

Joshua set this example by leading his house to serve the Lord (Joshua 24:15). Lois and Eunice also set this example as they discipled Timothy, so that from childhood, Timothy was familiar with the sacred writings that are able to lead one to salvation (2 Timothy 1:5; 3:14–15). It is clear that throughout Scripture, "God permeated family life" (Lawson, 2011, p. 77). This is a "God-given mandate" that finds Christian parents "cultivating a household environment where children grow to respect, love, and follow Jesus" (Ware, 2011, p. 69). Scripture provides many examples of parents who witnessed the transformational impact the Gospel can have as families believe in Jesus Christ (Luke 19:1–10; Acts 10:23–47; 16:11–15; 16:29–34; 2 Timothy 1:5). This life transformation extends to the entire family (Acts 2:39).

Bringing the Gospel Home

Just as one cannot overestimate the need families have for the Gospel or the impact the Gospel has on families, one cannot overestimate the opportunity parents have to bring the Gospel into the home. Scripture calls parents to teach the Word of God to their children, proclaiming testimonies of His Gospel, goodness, faithfulness, deliverance, and power (Genesis 18:19; Exodus 13:14; Deuteronomy 6:7–9; Deuteronomy 11:19–21; Joshua 4:6–7; Psalm 78:4–7; Psalm 145:4; Ephesians 6:4; 1 Peter 3:7).

In Christian Smith and Amy Adamczyk's research (2021), they examined American religious parents to determine the crucial trends that are present when faith is passed down from one generation to the next. At the heart of their conclusion was the recognition that parents have the greatest opportunity of putting the Gospel in front of their children: "The influence of parents on children while they still live at home—including their influence on their religious identities, beliefs, and practices—is paramount, lasting for years, decades, often lifetimes" (pp. 2–3). They added, "the influence of parents in religiousness trumps every other influence" (p. 3). With such an opportunity available to parents, Christian parents do well to bring the Gospel into the home, for, "Our homes are to be homes founded upon the Word of God. Our families are to be families that grow daily. Our mornings, afternoons, and evenings are to be spent teaching the Gospel, living the Gospel, modeling the Gospel, and proclaiming the Gospel" (Williams, 2015, p. 15).

Bringing the Gospel Into the Home Through Family Worship

Throughout Scripture and throughout church history, there is a long line of faithful examples of families who enjoyed the Gospel message together through family worship:

> Family worship takes place when a Christian household gathers to pray, teach the Word of God, and praise the Lord. Many families today seek to cultivate regular rhythms of family worship. In these homes, family worship becomes an intentional and joyful response to a biblical call, biblical commands, and biblical examples. Blessings await any family seeking to bring the Gospel into the home through family worship (Williams, 2021, p. 6).

As Andreas Köstenberger wrote, "God's express will for his people Israel is still His will for God's people in the church today. Christian parents have the mandate and serious obligation to instill their religious heritage in their children." Family worship—teaching the Scriptures, joint prayer, and joint praises—opens the door for Christian parents to pass down the Gospel message to their children and their children's children. This spiritual discipline has been championed throughout church history and is still put forth as one of the most effective ways to lead a household to know Jesus.

Puritan pastor, Richard Baxter, viewed family worship as God's will for the home and put forth an apologetic for all families to practice family worship. Baxter wrote, "If then there is no family whereof God is not the Father or Founder and the Master or Owner and Governor, then there is none but should honor and fear Him or worship Him, and that not only as single men but as families, because He is not only the Father and Master, the Lord and Ruler of them as men but also as families" (Baxter, 2010, p. 65). George Hamond seemed to agree with Baxter's call. Hamond considered family worship a discipline required by Scripture. He wrote, "Men are not at liberty whether they will worship God in their families or not" (2005, p. 17). Yet another Puritan, Matthew Henry, added his call for families to worship God together and teach His Word in their homes. Henry preached, "this is an excellent method ... to teach our children the things of God, by talking of them as we sit in the house, and go by the way, when we lie down, and when we rise up" (2007, p. 39).

Scholars, pastors, and authors today continue to put forth this call for family worship, recognizing the impact the Gospel can have on hearts and homes. Donald Whitney's book, *Family Worship*, reviewed the applicable Bible verses and a few examples of family worship throughout church history. Whitney then provided an exhortation for today's household. He wrote, "God deserves to be worshiped daily in our homes by our families" (2016, p. 51). Joel Beeke added his own encouragement for families today. He noted, "Given the importance of family worship as a potent force in winning untold millions to gospel truth throughout the ages, we ought not be surprised that God requires heads of households to do all they can to lead their families in worshiping the living God" (2009, p. 7).

Smith and Adamczyk's research (2021) revealed the impact weekly rhythms of family worship can have on the next generation. They contrasted a family that only engages in spiritual matters on Sunday mornings with a family that brings God's Word into the home throughout the week:

> Parents conversing with children about religion is a powerful signal to children of religion's personal importance. People usually talk about what they care about ... When all parents say about religion to children during a week is something like "Okay, everyone, leaving for church in thirty minutes," that is telling. When conversations immediately turn after religious worship services to nonreligious interests, that is telling, too. The message may be subliminal, but their accumulated socialization effects are powerful. By contrast, when parents talk naturally and substantively about religion and its place in life throughout the week, that effectively indicates to children that, in the mix of life's many priorities and values, this stuff matters a lot (p. 83).

Smith and Adamczyk's research highlight some of the ways spiritual engagement in the home can impact the next generation. The call for families to bring the Gospel into the home through family worship remains today, as do the blessings of family worship. Ken Coley and Blair Robinson reminded the reader of the transformational impact the Gospel has on homes today and the blessings discovered through family worship. They highlighted these blessings of family worship, and wrote, "God will be glorified, you will be sanctified, and your family will be blessed" (2021, p. 110).

Conclusion

The Gospel message woven throughout Scripture tells a story:

- God was with us: God's family created
- God came to us: God's family reborn, and
- God will be with us: God's family restored

Within this Gospel framework is a message about family and relationships, for we see the Gospel from the beginning of time as a story about marriage and family (Danylak, 2020, pp. 52–53). This is the story that still blesses homes today.

Families today remain in desperate need of the Gospel. The good news is that the Gospel of Christ continues to impact and transform families. One of the ways the Gospel impacts the home is through the biblical and historical practice of family worship. As families gather to teach the Word of God in the home and share joint prayers and praises, they enjoy the power of the Gospel as they grow closer to the Lord, growing together as a family.

The family of God, as it exists on the earth in the form of the church, will one day be restored to their rightful relationship with the Lord. Until then, let us delight in the Gospel of grace. Let us believe in the Gospel and proclaim it in our homes and beyond. Let us celebrate this good news message as we worship Christ together.

References

Bates, Matthew W. (2021). *The Gospel precisely: Surprisingly good news*. Copell, TX: Renew.org.

Bates, Matthew W. (2017). *Salvation by allegiance alone: Rethinking faith, works, and the Gospel of Jesus the king*. Grand Rapids: Baker Academic.

Baxter, R. (2010). *The godly home.* Wheaton, IL: Crossway.

Beeke, J. R. (2009). *Family worship.* Grand Rapids, MI: Reformation Heritage Books.

Cardoza, F. (2011). Crisis on the Doorstep. In M. Anthony & M. Anthony (Eds.) *A theology for family ministries*. Nashville, TN: B&H Academic.

Chandler, Diane J. (2014). *Christian spiritual formation: An integrated approach for personal and relational wholeness*. Downers Grove, IL: IVP Academic.

Coley, K. & Robinson, B. (2021). *Equipping fathers to lead family worship*. Nashville, TN: Randall House.

Danylak, Barry. (2010). *Redeeming singleness: How the storyline of Scripture affirms the single life.* Wheaton: IL: Crossway.

Enns, P. P. (1989). *The Moody handbook of theology*. Chicago, IL: Moody Press.

Goldingay, J. (2009). *Old Testament theology: Israel's life,* Volume Three. Downers Grove, IL: IVP Academic.

Grudem, W. (1994). *Systematic theology: An introduction to biblical doctrine.* Grand Rapids, MI: Zondervan.

Hamond, G. (2005). *The case for family worship*. Orlando, FL: Soli Deo Gloria Publications.

Hellerman, Joseph H. (2001). *The ancient church as family*. Minneapolis: Fortress.

Henry, M. with Brown, S. (Ed.). (2007). *A Church in the house: Restoring daily worship to the Christian household.* San Antonio, TX: The Vision Forum, INC.

Hugenberger, Gordon P. (1994). *Marriage as a covenant: Biblical law and ethics as developed from Malachi*. Eugene, OR: Wipf & Stock.

Hull, B. (2016). *Conversion and discipleship: You can't have one without the other.* Grand Rapids: Zondervan.

Köstenberger, A. J. & Jones, D. W. (2010). *God, marriage, and family: Rebuilding the biblical foundation.* Wheaton, IL: Crossway.

Lawson, M. S. (2011). Old Testament teachings on the family. In M. Anthony & M. Anthony (Eds.) *A theology for family ministries*. Nashville, TN: B&H Academic.

McKnight, S. (2016). *The king Jesus Gospel: The original good news revisited.* Grand Rapids: Zondervan.

Moon, JinHyoung. (2020). *An examination of the biblical characteristics of marriage as a paradigm of spiritual formation*. Fort Worth, TX: Southwestern Baptist Theological Seminary.

Nelson, B. & Jones, T. P. (2011). The problem with family ministry. In R. Stinson & T. P Jones (Eds.), *Trained in the Fear of God: Family Ministry in Theological, Historical, and Practical Perspective*. Grand Rapids, MI: Kregel Academic & Professional.

Patterson, Paige. (2012). *Revelation. The new American commentary*. Nashville: B&H.

Shirley, Chris. (2018). *Family ministry and the church: A leader's guide for ministry through families.* Nashville: Randall House Academic.

Smith, C. & Adamczyk, A. (2021). Handing down the faith: How parents pass their religion on to the next generation. Oxford: Oxford University Press.

Snodgrass, Klyne R. (2022). *You need a better Gospel: Reclaiming the good news of participation with Christ*. Grand Rapids: Baker Academic.

Ware, B. A. (2011). The Father, the Son, and the Holy Spirit: The trinity as theological foundation for family ministry. In R. Stinson & T. P Jones (Eds.), *Trained in the fear of God: Family ministry in theological, historical, and practical perspective*. Grand Rapids, MI: Kregel Academic & Professional.

Whitney, D. (2016). *Family worship*. Wheaton, IL: Crossway.

Williams, J. (2015). *Gospel family: Cultivating family discipleship, family worship, & family missions.* Houston, TX: Lucid Books.

Williams, J. (2021) *A practical theology of family worship: Richard Baxter's timeless encouragement for today's home*. Grand Rapids, MI: Reformation Heritage Books.

Authors Biography

Chris Shirley, Ph.D., is the dean of the Terry School of Educational Ministries at Southwestern Baptist Theological Seminary. Dr. Shirley, author of *Family Ministry and the Church: A Leader's Guide to Ministry through the Family* (2018, Randall House) also teaches in the areas of discipleship and family ministry.

Jonathan Williams, Ph.D., is the executive director of Gospel Family Ministries and the author of the books *A Practical Theology of Family Worship* (2021) and *Gospel Family* (2015). He also teaches as an adjunct professor at Southwestern Baptist Theological Seminary and is the managing editor of the *Southwestern D6 Family Ministry Journal.*

Challenges to Passing on the Faith to Families with Special Needs Children

Major Matthew McCraney, D.Min.

Abstract: Families with special needs children appear largely absent from churches relative to their percentage of the population. These families often feel unwelcome and misunderstood, sometimes leading to a rejection of church and the faith. To address passing on faith to the next generation of special needs families, churches need to cultivate a cultural change. This includes intentional repudiation of the moral model of disability in all its practical forms, understanding the limitations of sensory and other physical obstacles in the learning environment, and cultivating partnerships with parents to address unique challenges to participating in the ministries of the church.

Recognizing the Need

The prevalence of children with special needs among families in the United States has increased significantly in recent years. This increase is due in part to better diagnostic tools and an increase in awareness of developmental conditions (Samadi, et al., 2022). However, families with special needs children appear largely absent from churches relative to their percentage of the population. Scholars across the theological and philosophical spectrum agree with this observation (Hardwick, 2021; Hubach, 2020; Brock, 2020; Yong, 2011; Beates & Tada, 2012). Additionally, many of the most popular approaches to family ministry make little or no mention of families with special needs (Kimmel, 2013; Rienow, 2013; Jones, 2019; Kim & Tidwell, 2020; Rainer, 2005; Macchia, 1999; Shirley, 2018;

Ross, 2017). Families with special needs children often feel unwelcome and misunderstood, sometimes leading to a rejection of church and the faith.

To address this constraint to passing on faith to the next generation of special needs families, churches need to cultivate a cultural change within their communities. This includes intentional repudiation of the moral model of disability in all its practical forms, understanding the limitations of sensory and other physical obstacles in the learning environment, and cultivating partnerships with parents to address unique challenges to participating in the ministries of the church. These represent the necessary philosophical first steps that serve as precursors to an effective ministry to special needs families and the passing on of the faith tradition.

Special Needs Families: How Do We Understand Disability?

Before diving into solutions and applications, one must understand the nature of disability and how it affects special needs families. If simply accommodating special needs families was sufficient, many more of them would attend church on a regular basis and the barrier to passing on the faith would be reduced. Brian Brock noted that the issue of accommodation has largely been achieved in the United States, so this absence requires another explanation (2020, p. 1). This suggests that the issues keeping special needs families from church have more to do with the philosophy of the church culture, rather than accommodations. Jumping to applications without examining these underlying issues thoroughly can lead to insufficient and ineffective solutions.

It is necessary to unpack the idea of disability and answer the question, what makes a child special needs? Defining disability can be difficult, especially with the fast-paced change in language and social norms. Throughout history, disability and disfunction were viewed quite different than the modern era. Christian Laes suggested in *Disability in Antiquity* that while impairments and physically limiting conditions existed throughout the history of humanity, social forces either enable or disable a person (2020, p. 4). This essentially means that the society dictates what constitutes disability by its presuppositions, making a concise definition of disability somewhat of a moving target. The United Nations defines a disability in their discussion on the observance of *Persons with Disabilities Day* as,

> A condition or function judged to be significantly impaired relative to the usual standard of an individual of their group. The term is often used to refer to individual functioning, including physical impairment, sensory impairment, cognitive impairment, intellectual impairment, mental illness, and various types of chronic disease (United Nations, n.d.).

This definition demonstrates Laes' contention, as it defines disability in relation to the normative state of most humans.

Yong also provided a helpful word of caution from the biblical perspective on disabilities. He reminded Christians:

> There is no straightforward biblical notion that captures what the term *disability* has come to mean presently. Hence we need to keep in mind that our exploration of "the Bible and disability" needs to proceed with caution, so that we don't read too much of our present understanding into the biblical text (2011, p.6).

Since the category of disability does not appear in the Scriptures, interpreters must be careful in reading the category into larger narratives. This understanding weighs on the interpretations of such passages as John 5:14 and 1 Corinthians 11:27–30 addressed below.

For the purpose of this work, disability will be defined as an impairment, whether physical, mental, or emotional that limits functioning in society in a significant way. While this definition cannot be considered complete or all encompassing, sometimes the simpler the definition allows the greatest amount of discussion. Disabilities exist in space and time, not merely as social constructs or moral judgments. A special needs child is one who has one or more conditions that could be classified as a disability under the above definition.

Also critical to this discussion is understanding that the current state of special needs families being absent from the church is a relatively recent development. Throughout the history of the church, care for those whom we would classify disabled stood as a hallmark of the church. For instance, Augustine saw this care as central to the spiritual growth of his community (2016, p. 338). Augustine went so far as to include in his list of disabilities and infirmities, numerous "defects of the mind," such as excessive lusts, proclivity toward anger, timidity, forgetfulness, and intellectual impairment (2016, p. 329).

The practices of the monastic orders during the early first millennia mirrored Augustine's approach, mandating the care for those with disabilities. (2016, p. 352). The period that followed in the Eastern Roman empire demonstrated a similar level of care and concern as Stephanos Efthymiadis noted and wrote, "Leaving disabled people to their fate was no longer regarded as permissible, as it had been in Greek and Roman Antiquity" (2016, p. 399). Contrary to the Greek and Roman understanding that saw the disabled as worthy of discard and death, the Christian community saw them as worthy of life and care due to their Christian convictions. This view persisted through the Reformation. Therefore, the reemergence of the moral model of disability within Christian thought stands against the tradition of the orthodox Christian faith.

The Moral Model of Disability

The moral model of disability represents one of the greatest challenges to those with special needs children and one of the greatest departures from orthodox Christin practice in the modern church. It supposes, much like Job's friends and Jesus' disciples (John 9), that disabilities result from sinful behavior either in the parent or the child (McNair, 2015, pp. 10–15). Intrinsic to most viewpoints throughout history, whether explicitly or implicitly lies the connection of disability to sin. As Edgar Kellenberger rightly stated, "Notions about the relation of sin to sickness and disability are lurking in the archaic depths of the human soul" (2016, p. 58). Kristi Upson-Saia pointed out paradoxically that while disability was inextricably linked to sin or disfunction, virtually everyone suffered from some sort of physical impairment (2011, p. 94). In fact, she argued most people in the ancient world held a physiognomic view, which attributed desirable characteristics with virtue and undesirable features with depravity (2011, p. 101). This view persists in many parts of the world (McNair, 2015, p. 11).

This ancient idea has not been completely excised from Christian thought. As a modern example, Michael Beates who has a paralyzed daughter related that "well-intentioned but theologically obtuse believers have sincerely asked us if we had confessed the sin in our lives that must surely be responsible for her affliction" (2012, introduction). The assumption made is that their sins or parenting decisions were the direct cause of their child's condition. Much to the dismay of many with special needs children, this works-based viewpoint remains prevalent in the church in various forms.

While the moral model was the primary understanding throughout history, many vestiges of it remain throughout the world and in church. Modern proponents of the veracity of the moral model have touted John 5:14 as proof (Eiesland, 1994, p. 74), noting that Jesus told a disabled man to "Sin no more, that nothing worse may happen to you" (ESV). For instance, Jay Adams took the position that John 5:14 suggests the man's sin led to his disability (1986, p. 109). However, as Gerald Borchert rightly argued, "These words are not meant to be a cause-and-effect statement related to his sickness or paralysis. Such a direct identification between personal sin and illness, which was proposed by the disciples in the story of the blind man (John 9:2), was firmly rejected by Jesus (John 9:3)" (1996, p. 235). George Beasley-Murray agreed noting that John 9:3 forbids such a connection (1987, p. 74). Adams also pointed to 1 Corinthians 11:27–30 to justify a connection between disability and sin (1986, p. 110). However, as Mark Taylor rightly observed, this passage (1 Corinthians 11:27–30) should be seen as a corporate punishment on the church for their sinful actions, similar to the plagues against Israel, rather than as a cause-and-effect transaction (2014, p. 277). Interestingly, Adams's view shares more in common with the Medieval Roman Catholic view of disability, finding its cause in sin, rather than the biblical worldview (Metzler, 2016, p. 465).

The Moral Model of Disability and PTSD

Another example of the moral model can be seen in how the church addresses conditions such as Post-Traumatic Stress Disorder (PTSD), which is classified as a disability. Some biblical counseling material addresses PTSD by stating that any persisting fear after the danger has passed is a sinful response that questions the goodness of God (Asher & Asher,

2004, p. 152). In some cases, they question the salvation of the suffering due to their struggle (Asher & Asher, 2004, p. 152). As someone who regularly counsels those who suffer from PTSD, I find this position abhorrent and unbiblical as it places moral culpability on individuals for physical responses beyond their control. PTSD is primarily a physiological condition in which the stress hormones activate and remain activated due to a shock to the system and has nothing to do with the faith of the individual (Kolk, 2014, p. 30). The response of some in the Christian community connecting this disability to sin betray a moral-model-of-disability way of thinking.

The Moral Model of Disability and ASD

The moral model of disability finds expression in various other places within the Christian community as well. Some are more obvious, such Beates's example mentioned above, that finds parents being asked if they had repented of their sins that caused a child's disability. Others are more subtle. A telling example lies in the debate over vaccination and its supposed connection to Autism Spectrum Disorder (ASD).

A belief commonly held among the United States population is that vaccines hold a causal link to Autism Spectrum Disorder (ASD). Gallup found in 2015 that 10% of the United States population still believe vaccines cause ASD, while 46% are "unsure," even though this theory was thoroughly disproven a decade ago (Hornig, et al., 2008). The assumption of casual link often occurs because the approximate age at which many children are diagnosed coincides with the ages certain vaccines are administered. In the Gallup study only a minority of the population believed the numerous studies that clearly disprove the link between vaccines and ASD.

The 46% who were "unsure" in the study is particularly alarming. While one in ten who firmly believe this theory may seem to suggest only a fringe, though not a statistically insignificant belief, only 45% of the population firmly held that vaccines were not responsible, suggesting that a majority sees either a link or the possibility of a link between a parental decision and ASD (Reinhart, 2020). Parents of children with ASD receive criticism for their choice to vaccinate, spurred on by untrustworthy websites that perpetuate false beliefs. Yet this statistic illustrates only one piece of the parental "blame game." Numerous other beliefs about the cause of ASD have gained traction in the cultural conversation and most of these beliefs indict the parent's action or inaction, whether knowingly or unknowingly, for their child's resulting condition. The research mentioned above suggests parents of children with ASD face presumption of fault from a significant percentage of the population, which is an example of the moral model of disability.

Even among the ASD community, various explanations for the neurological condition abound, though usually they share the causal agent ultimately as parental action or inaction. This remains the case even as the best, most recent evidence suggests a genetic cause rather than an action or environmental agent (Baron-Cohen, 2004). Most experts see genetic links to outbreak rather than environment causes. Proposed, though scientifically unproven causes range from a lack of attachment at early developmental ages (a clear indictment of parental action/ inaction) to sugar and gluten consumption (Autism Science Foundation, n.d.). Toxins in the air, chemicals in the food, medicines consumed during pregnancy, and parental behavior have all been suggested to have possible connections to ASD. Helen Tager-Flusberg, professor of psychological and brain sciences at Boston University and director of the Center for Autism Research Excellence, eloquently illustrated the detrimental effect this has on parents. She stated:

> Too many women still hear from professionals, family and friends that perhaps they did or didn't do something that caused their child to have autism. Many of the parents who have participated in our research over the years carry profound guilt about their child's condition even when no one has directly accused them of contributing to it … So it is no wonder some parents feel as if they're to blame—in one way or another—for their children's autism (2020).

Both internal pressures and external societal assumptions shape an environment for parents where intense feelings of guilt can go unchecked. Misunderstandings of research and the statements of high profile and powerful people influence the way parents see their actions related to their child with ASD.

The Effects of the Moral Model of Disability on the Church and Families

Often, these beliefs find expression in moral terms, hence betraying the moral model of disability mindset that sin lies at the heart of disability. It is not uncommon for parents of special needs children to hear statements in the church such as, "We didn't vaccinate our children because we trusted God's perfectly designed immune system." This mindset expands beyond vaccines and often finds its way into questions of birthing practices. Again, it is not uncommon to hear comments related to the health of a child based on the birthing technique (i.e. epidural use vs. "natural," home vs. hospital, vaginal vs. cesarean section) often expressed in moral terms.

From comments on parental health choices to outright assumption of disability as punishment, these represent just a few ways that the moral model infiltrates the Christian mindset and pushes families with disabilities away from the church. Suffice it to say, in the modern period within the church, guilt and shame find themselves attached to the disabled and their caretakers through a furtherance of the moral model. Like a hideous distraction, the moral model of disability still appears in even the most Gospel-centered communities. If we hope to pass on the faith to families with special needs children, leaders must address the theological misconceptions and misunderstandings inherent in the moral model of disability and they must correct errant teachings quickly. Such correction opens the door for the church to minister to these families in new, helpful, biblical, and loving ways. It is a difficult and rewarding ministry. As Irene Cheung wrote:

> Serving families of children with ASD requires perseverance, just as the parents have to endure multiple stressors to continue to bring up their children. It is a life long journey to walk with them as they transition into various life stages, each with different challenges. The amount of work and commitment involved in devoting manpower and resources to these families with children with ASD can be huge and intense, but it is worthy work for God's kingdom and can be accomplished by God's grace (2019, pp. 75–76).

Sensory Issues and Understanding

To address passing on faith to the next generation of special needs families, churches not only need an intentional repudiation of the moral model of disability in all its practical forms, but also an understanding of the limitations of sensory and other physical obstacles in the learning environment. As an Army family, we change duty stations frequently and every few years we begin the arduous task of finding a new church. While theology and right practice rank number one in our decision, because we have a special needs child other considerations factor prominently as well. For instance, our most recent church had no carpeting and no acoustic sound absorption on the walls, leading to a significant reverb effect in the room. We could not seem to figure out why our son became increasingly agitated during the service, when at our prior church he had no issues. One week we had to watch the service from an auxiliary room and noticed he had no issue sitting through the service. A sensory issue led to him being incredibly uncomfortable and he felt he had to get out of the room.

Sensory issues can be challenging for special needs families as seemingly small details like room acoustics can cause significant issues. However, the response of church members to those sensory issue reactions can cause even more problems if they do not understand how the child is being impacted. Parents often find it difficult to go unnoticed in ways parents of neuro-typical children can easily take for granted. Children with sensory issues draw attention in public situations through symptoms that often present as behavior issues in need of discipline rather than an external sign of disability (i.e. blindness, wheelchair use, hearing aids, etc.; Hendrickson, 2009, p. 33). Outside observations of sensory "meltdowns," which result from any number of external or internal agitations, can appear, to unknowing family, friends, church members, or bystanders, as a lack of parental discipline.

Compounding this issues, popular Christian parenting models lack understanding of unique issues of discipline related to children with disabilities. Disciplinary methods found in books such as *Shepherding a Child's Heart* (Tripp, 1995) give no exceptions for physical discipline, regardless of disability, history of abuse in foster or adopted children, or any other complicating issue. In many disciplinary approaches advocated in Christian circles, a works-based approach dominates all other concerns. In numerous issues related to parenting, what works for the neuro-typical child does not necessarily work for special needs children.

Some parents express great distress at comments from judgmental individuals, inadvertent actions (i.e. lack of eye contact during problematic behavior, shunning, etc.), and misinterpretations of their child's maladaptive behaviors (i.e. Church members standing aghast when my son shouts at the end of the sermon, "Finally, it's over!"). A child's response to sensory issues too often is confused for behavioral issues, leading to feelings of shame and isolation. Many parents end up rejecting the church as they feel the church has rejected them.

Ultimately, many church members do not understand how overwhelming the sensory issue can be to the special needs child. They do not understand that the child is not fidgeting or stemming out of disrespect for the church, but because they feel every seam on their clothes as if it were burning into their skin or hear every word as if it were blared through a 100-watt amp inches from their face. Smells that annoy the average person can cause nausea in the special needs child. These issues should not be dismissed as behavioral issues.

Further compounding feelings of rejection are the responses of church members when worship services are disrupted by sensory issues (Plaats, 2019, pp. 43–47). ASD for example usually presents with socially disruptive behaviors such as stimming (uncontrollable and unconscious, repetitive movements such as "flapping" of hands, walking on the balls of one's feet, and exaggerated extremity movements) and meltdowns (Hendrickson, 2009, p. 62). Additionally, there are significant neurological comorbidities including epilepsy, sleep disorders, and motor delay/impairment which impact social functioning (Jeste, 2011). McNair and Rhodes captured this situation perfectly in noting:

> There can be additional demands for attention, funding, and time, and these can be severely emotionally draining. Sometimes marriages struggle. Those of us looking on from the outside might be tempted to say things like, 'raising a child with a disability can be very difficult. The child with the disability is the reason that family is struggling.' In this way, we do nothing

> to help—and then blame the child with the disability for the family's experience (2020, pp. 44–75).

The apparent problem to outsiders become either the parent's action/inaction or the child's deficit in social functioning. Attention often falls on parents who otherwise would go unnoticed had their child been neurotypical. All of this attention creates an environment where families with special needs children feel unwelcomed and isolated. Instead of burdening parents with blame, guilt, or shame, churches would do well to seek to understand the limitations of sensory and other physical obstacles while developing partnerships with parents of special needs children.

Cultivating Partnerships With Parents

To address passing on faith to the next generation of special needs families, churches need to cultivate partnerships with parents to address unique challenges to participating in the ministries of the church. A lack of intentional, prayerful, and supportive partnership from the church can invalidate or minimize the struggle of the special needs family. Such partnerships may require renewed focus on the part of the church as modern church culture tends to deny the reality of brokenness and cover over signs of weakness (Beates, 2012).

When a parent shares that their child has a special need or any condition not immediately noticeable, the frequent responses include, "I would have never known," "She seems completely normal," or even, "Really! Are you sure?" The message, admittedly meant as a compliment, echoes in the ears of the parent: "You have hidden your brokenness well." While this may result in momentary comfort, it does nothing to validate the experience of the family who struggles with this unique weakness and offers no grace or comfort in the midst of their weakness. Congregations need to be taught to recognize special needs families and show grace rather than judgement. This gracious recognition of their brokenness, weaknesses, and needs become the initial steps to cultivating a partnership with these families.

Practical Suggestions

Integrating special needs families into the life of the church so the faith can be passed on to the next generation requires understanding and listening. It requires a theological and philosophical gut check. Church leaders can lead the way through numerous practical, though potentially painful steps.

First, leaders should examine their own philosophical and theological presuppositions. When seeing a child with an apparent behavior problem or developmental issue, does he or she assume the parent is to blame because of some deficiency in their parenting? What assumptions emerge when assessing the situation? Often leaders only see the externals, not the underlying issue. By examining and acknowledging one's own assumptions, we can learn to be more compassionate to these families. This opens the door to meaningful conversations and compassionate engagements modeled by leaders, rather than assumptions regarding the spiritual condition of the families. We do well to remember that Jesus constantly challenged the assumptions of those around Him, especially His disciples (John 9:1–3; Luke 13:1–5, etc.).

Hard questions and honest reflection should follow this self-examination for church leaders and members. Perhaps the first question to consider is whether or not there are special needs families present in the congregation. If so, church leaders can ask them if they are made to feel welcome or do they feel like an outsider or isolated by the church culture? If there are not any special needs families present, church leaders need to evaluate the potential reasons for their absence. What are the practices and attitudes that may hinder the special needs family's entrance into the community? These admittedly hard questions need answers if the church aims to reach special needs families.

Leaders should also avoid a transactional approach to God in teaching. My family once attended a chapel service with our autistic son. During the service he became agitated and I sat with him outside the sanctuary, calming him with his service dog. I listened as the pastor preached a sermon around the idea that if people just had enough faith, God would heal them. I could not help but wonder where our healing was or whether we just did not have enough faith. As someone with a theological education, I knew the pastor's error in seeing God in such transactional terms. However, what about those who do not know any better and doubt their faith, or worse, doubt God, because they have not received healing?

Transactional approaches to God abound within Christian culture. This proves inconsistent with the biblical example. God did not promise Isaiah worldly success for faithfulness, but that his ministry would seem unfruitful (Isaiah 6:11–12). John the Baptist's reward for faithfulness was death (Mark 6:27–28). Throughout Scripture, one finds many examples of faithful men and women suffering physically (e.g., Acts 7:54–60; 12:1–5; 16:19–24; 21:30–33). The Bible is full of faithful servants who did not experience healing or physical reward. Why should we expect any different?

Finally, leaders should encourage the church to listen to special needs families. Those with disabilities experience life differently due to their conditions. Listening to their struggles without trite cliché comments allows the individual to truly be seen and heard. Often, those with disabilities are ignored because their condition makes us uncomfortable as it forces us to acknowledge our own weaknesses. In an effort not to be rude, some parents teach their children not to stare at those who are different. That habit carries on into adulthood, potentially causing isolation. Listen to those who struggle without judgement or assumption so they feel comfortable in our gatherings.

Conclusion

Those with disabilities and their families are often missing from church due to isolation. The church's underlying presuppositions and philosophical approaches can have a significant impact on this people group, hindering the church's ability to reach the next generation. Leaders must continually ask whether their approaches honor God and rightly handle His word. Otherwise, people with disabilities and their families will continue to feel unwelcomed in many churches.

On the other hand, a welcoming and loving church can find new opportunities to support special needs families and to help pass on faith to the next generation. Cheung also recognized this opportunity. Cheung concluded, "It is important for every church to reach out to those with disabilities and their families, showing acceptance as modeled by Jesus in welcoming the underprivileged group to His great banquet. The purpose is to allow these families and the church congregation to walk life journeys together as a compassionate community" (2019, p. 75).

References

Adams, J. E. (1986). *Competent to Counsel: Introduction to Nouthetic Counseling.* The Jay Adams Library. Grand Rapids, MI: Ministry Resources Library.

Asher, M. & Asher, M. (2004). *The Christian's guide To psychological terms*. Bemidji, MN: Focus Pub.

Baron-Cohen, S. (2004). The cognitive neuroscience of autism. *Journal of Neurology, Neurosurgery & Psychiatry*; 75: 945–948.

Beasley-M. & Raymond, G. (1987). *John*. Word Biblical Commentary, 36. Dallas, TX: Word Books.

Beates, M. S. & Eareckson-Tada, J. (2012). *Disability and the Gospel: How God uses our brokenness to display His grace*. Wheaton, IL: Crossway.

Borchert, G. L. (1996). *John 1–11*, Volume 25A, The New American Commentary. Nashville, TN: Broadman & Holman Publishers.

Brock, B. R. (2020). *Wondrously wounded: Theology, disability, and the body of Christ.* Waco, TX: Baylor University Press.

Brock, B. & Swinton, J. (Eds.), (2012). *Disability in the Christian tradition: A reader*. Grand Rapids, MI: William B. Eerdmans Pub. Co.

Cheung, I. (2019). Understanding and supporting parents of children with autism in coping with stressors related to the diagnostic process. *D6 Family Ministry Journal, Volume 4*, 65–80.

Eiesland, N. L. (1994). *The disabled God: Toward a liberatory theology of disability*. Nashville, TN: Abingdon Press.

Reinhart, R. J. (2020). Fewer in U.S. continue to see vaccines as important. Retrieved from https://news.gallup.com/poll/276929/fewer-continue-vaccines-important.aspx.

Hardwick, L. (2021). *Disability and the church: A vision for diversity and inclusion.* Downers Grove, IL: IVP.

Hendrickson, L. (2009). *Finding Your child's way on the autism spectrum.* Chicago, IL: Moody.

Hubach, S. O. (2020). *Same lake, different boat: Coming alongside people touched by disability, revised and updated.* Phillipsburg, NJ: P&R Publishing.

Jeste, S. S. (2011). The neurology of autism spectrum disorders. *Current Opinion in Neurology 24, no. 2* (April): 132–39. Retrieved from http://dx.doi.org/10.1097/wco.0b013e3283446450.

Jones, R. D, Kellen, K. L., & Green, R. (2021). *The Gospel for disordered lives: An introduction to Christ-centered biblical counseling*. Nashville, TN: B&H Academic.

Jones, T. P. (2019). *Perspectives on family ministry: 3 views*. Nashville, TN: B & H Publishing Group.

Kim, J. J. & Tidwell, C. (Eds.), (2020). *The educational ministry of a church, second edition: A comprehensive model for students and ministers, comprehensive edition*. Nashville, TN: B&H Academic.

Kimmel, T. (2013). *Connecting church & home, 1st edition.* Nashville, TN: Randall House.

Laes, C. (Ed.), (2020). *Disability in antiquity. Rewriting antiquity*. New York, NY: Routledge.

Macchia, S. (1999). *Becoming a healthy church: Ten traits of a vital ministry.* Grand Rapids, MI: Baker Books.

McNair, J. (2015). Disability and human supports. *Christian Journal for Global Health 2, no. 2*, 10–15.

McNair, J., & Rhodes, B. (2020). Social healing: Cultural change as an alternative to the devaluation of persons with disabilities. *Journal of the Christian Institute on Disability, 9(1)*, 44–75. Retrieved from https://journal.joniandfriends.org/index.php/jcid/article/view/225.

Melcher, S. J., Parsons, M. C., & Yong, A. (Eds.), (2017). *The Bible and disability: A commentary*. Waco, TX: Baylor University Press.

Rainer, T. (2005). *Breakout churches: Discover how to make the leap*. Grand Rapids, MI: Zondervan.

Rob Rienow, R. (2013). *Limited church: Unlimited kingdom; Uniting church and family in the great commission*. Nashville, TN: Randall House.

Ross, R. (2017). *Youth ministry that lasts a lifetime*. Fort Worth, TX: Seminary Hill Press.

Samadi, S. A., Biçak, C. A., Noori, H., Abdalla, B., Abdullah, A., & Ahmed, L. (2022). Autism spectrum disorder diagnostic criteria changes and impacts on the diagnostic scales-utility of the 2nd and 3rd versions of the Gilliam Autism Rating Scale (GARS). *Brain Sciences* (2076–3425) 12 (5): 537. doi:10.3390/brainsci12050537.

Schumm, D. Y., & Stoltzfus, M. (Eds.), (2011). *Disability in Judaism, Christianity, and Islam: Sacred texts, historical traditions, and social analysis*. New York, NY: Palgrave Macmillan.

Shirley, C. (2018). *Family ministry and the church: A leader's guide for ministry through families*. Nashville, TN: Randall House Publications.

Tager-Flusberg, H. (2020). Should scientists study mothers of children with autism? *Spectrum Autism Research News*. Retrieved from https://www.spectrumnews.org/opinion/viewpoint/should-scientists-study-mothers-of-children-with-autism/.

Taylor, M. (2014). *1 Corinthians*, In E. R. Clendenen, (Ed.), The New American Commentary, Volume 28. Nashville, TN: B&H Publishing Group.

Tripp, T. (1995). *Shepherding a child's heart*. Wapwallopen, PA: Shepherd Press.

Van Der Kolk, B. (2014). The body keeps the score: *Brain, mind, and body in the healing of trauma, 1st edition*. London: Penguin Books.

Vander Plaats, D. (2019). A dissonant witness. *Journal of the Christian Institute on Disability 8, no. 1*, 43–47.

Yong, A. (2011). *The Bible, disability, and the church: A new vision of the people of God*. Grand Rapids, MI: William B. Eerdmans Publishing Company.

Yong, A. (2007). Theology and down syndrome: Reimagining disability in late modernity. Waco, TX: Baylor University Press.

Author Biography

Matthew McCraney, D.Min., is a chaplain (Major) in the U.S. Army and serves as the senior chaplain for 7th Special Forces Group. He holds a D.Min. from Southeastern Baptist Theological Seminary and is a Ph.D. candidate at Southwestern Baptist Theological Seminary. He is married with four children, one with special needs.

Family Ministry and Theology: A Theological Reflection on Three Church of England Congregations

Gareth Crispin, Ph.D.

Abstract: Although theology does not automatically lead to practice it does provide a foundation for practice, with certain types of theology providing fertile ground for particular types of practice. Classically Reformed doctrines of the Trinity, Spirit, Church, and Scripture, along with commensurate understandings of leadership and views of youth and children provide theological foundations that may cohere with the development of family ministry in practice. In considering their church's theology, readers may be able to discern reasons why implementing family ministry is more or less difficult in their context and explore possible ways in which to develop family ministry in their setting.

Introduction

A number of writers have considered the theological foundations for family ministry (Anthony & Anthony, 2011; Stinson & Jones, 2011; Jones 2009). In particular, Old Testament (Lawson, 2011) and New Testament (Melick, 2011) teachings have been applied to family ministry as well as some particular systematic categories such as the Trinity (Ware, 2011). This article couples these previous works on family ministry with findings from a doctoral research project. The research project examined three Church of England congregations and a subsequent theological reflection on the themes that arose.

After defining terms and setting out the background to the research project, this article will suggest that while it is not possible to prove that doctrine leads to practice, it is possible to suggest that certain theological commitments are coherent and commensurate with certain practices and models of ministry. In particular, more classically reformed, conservative theological positions may provide fertile ground for family ministry when compared to less conservative theologies that might provide foundations that could more naturally cohere with intergenerational ministry. Those wishing to think more deeply about fostering family ministry within their churches may benefit from reflecting on the theological foundations of their churches and considering how those foundations may be helping or hindering the development of family ministry.

Definitions

For the purposes of this article, *family ministry* will be defined as "The process of intentionally and persistently coordinating a ministry's proclamation and practices so that parents are acknowledged, trained and held accountable as primary disciple-makers in their children's lives" (Jones, 2009, p. 40). While it is possible to further sub-divide family ministry (Jones, 2009), those more granular distinctions are not the concern of this paper. Instead, this paper will present *intergenerational ministry* as a somewhat contrasting model. Intergenerational ministry takes place when a congregation brings "the generations together in mutual serving, sharing, or learning within the core activities of the church in order to live out being the body of Christ to each other and the greater community" (Allen & Ross, 2012, p. 17). These definitions find family ministry focusing on the home as well as the action of parents and adults toward youth and children. It is in part necessarily vertical and top-down. The focus in intergenerational ministry, on the other hand, is the church and the action of all, regardless of age, toward each other. This approach implies a more horizontal or bottom-up approach.

Background to the Research Project

The conclusions of this paper are in part drawn from reflections on doctoral research that considered three Church of England congregations. In practice, the Church of England embraces a variety of theological positions. Graham Kings uses the idea of watercourses to distinguish between what are commonly called Conservative, Open, and Charismatic Evangelicals (Kings, 2003). Kings labels Conservative Evangelicals in the Church of England as the canals in that their overriding commitment to the Bible maintains a significant degree of stability in doctrine and practice. Open Evangelicals are then labelled rivers due to their more fluid approach to doctrine and practice. Lastly, Kings calls Charismatic Evangelicals the rapids because of their focus on an active continuationist pneumatology.

Within the research project, St. James (and its Minister, Bobby) was a clearly and committedly Open Evangelical church. St. Mary's (along with its Minister, Henry) was equally committed to a Charismatic Evangelical stance. Finally, St. Theresa's was mixed, with some Open, some Charismatic, and a few Conservative Evangelical voices.[1] The author's background is Conservative Evangelical and will provide some more anecdotal reflections on the more conservative position.

Findings From the Research Project

The findings from the research project suggested that family ministry and intergenerational ministries may be founded on contrasting theological positions. As can be seen in the definitions above, intergenerational ministry has a focus on mutuality that is not a chief feature of family ministry and equally family ministry has a focus on authority, hierarchy, and accountability that is less present in intergenerational ministry. Allen Harkness's proposed four constituent factors of intergenerational ministry emphasize the point; he sees mutuality between participants, collaboration, shared experiences, and bi-directional teaching as the heart of intergenerational ministry. The research project, though limited in scope, showed that where churches embraced intergenerational ministry, they did so by embracing values that are commensurate with these factors. The research project suggested that these values were promoted by more Open and Charismatic theological positions. Lastly, the research project also sug-

[1] Each church was treated as a separate case study. Documentary analysis, observations, and interviews with a range of church members, including youth and children were used as tools to analyze each case study.

gested that the reverse might also be true; that Open and Charismatic Evangelical churches are unlikely to be positively pre-disposed to family ministry. This aligns with the experience of the author within Conservative Evangelicalism, where a focus on family ministry is more prevalent than intergenerational ministry.[2] The way in which different theological positions support intergenerational ministry or family ministry can be explored through some key systematic categories, including: the Trinity, Spirit and church, leadership, Scripture and revelation, and the view of the next generation. In each case the focus on the vertical that is a feature of more conservative theology is seen as a possible reason for the focus on family ministry over and above intergenerational ministry.

Trinity

Bruce Ware has put forth the Trinity as a theological foundation for a certain view of family ministry. He argued that the Trinity:

> Provides us a model in which we understand the members of a family as fully equal in their value and dignity as human beings made in God's image. Yet each member has distinct roles and relationships within the family; these roles and relationships are worked out within an authority-submission structure that God designed as purposefully reflective of God himself (Ware, 2011, p. 67).

Ware's position on the Trinity begins with God as one, with a focus on essence of God and moves then to stress the eternal hierarchy within the Trinity: The Father sends the Son, and both then send the Spirit. The Trinity then provides us a model in which we understand the members of a family as fully equal in their value and dignity as human beings made in God's image. Yet each member has distinct roles and relationships within

[2] This is not to suggest that Conservative Evangelical churches cannot focus on intergenerational ministry (one suggestion for how Conservative Evangelical churches can embrace intergenerational ministry can be found in Crispin, 2018), nor that Open and Charismatic Evangelical Churches cannot work along family ministry lines, only that their theologies provide fertile ground for one and not the other. This is also not to suggest that intergenerational ministry and family ministry cannot be brought together (for a framework on how to bring intergenerational ministry and family ministry together see Crispin, 2019).

the family; these roles and relationships are worked out within an authority-submission structure that God designed as purposefully reflective of God himself.

Intergenerational ministry writers (including those, like Kenda Creasy Dean, who do not use that title but advocate many of the same practices and values) only mention the Trinity in passing (see for example Harkness, 2012, p. 126; Allen and Ross, 2012, pp. 111–113; Kang, 2011, p. 329; Dean, 2004, pp. 130–131 & 2010, p. xiv). Where they do talk of the Trinity, the focus is on the implications of the equal relationships between the persons of the Trinity rather than the hierarchy and difference between them.

In the research project Open and Charismatic church leaders identified Jurgen Moltmann as a significant influence in their ministries; this is perhaps unsurprising when Moltmann's views of the Trinity are considered.[3] Moltmann rejects the Western focus on the oneness of God (beginning with the one God and a focus on essence) and instead draws on the Eastern tradition, beginning with the three persons of the Trinity and (similarly to intergenerational ministry writers) a move away from God as substance and subject to God as relationship (Moltmann, 1981, p. 19).

In stark contrast to Ware's clear appreciation for the authority-submission structure, Moltmann's social Trinity leads him instead to conceive church governance more in terms of "relationship and community and participation" where "authority and obedience are replaced by dialogue, consensus, and harmony" (Moltmann, 1981, p. 202). It is not difficult to see how a social model of the Trinity as espoused by more Open and Charismatic Evangelicals provides a good theological grounding for those advocating for the mutual discursive approaches to intergenerational ministry.

As already mentioned, a definite causal link between theology and practice cannot be proven, but the way in which theology provides fertile ground for one or another practice is clear. Hierarchical, Western, Reformed positions on the Trinity are commensurate with family ministry,

[3]Moltmann would not identify himself as Open or Charismatic Evangelical but there are significant areas of common ground (see for example, Lord, 2003).

just as social, egalitarian models of the Trinity cohere more with intergenerational ministry.[4]

The Holy Spirit and the Church

Moltmann's view of the Spirit can again be set in contrast to more traditional Reformed positions. For Moltmann, the Spirit is a freer more active person of the Trinity than as seen within more Reformed positions and in being so makes the Trinity immanently open to creation (Moltmann, 1981, pp. 160–1). Not only is the Spirit seemingly not tied to the sending of the Father and the Son in the same way as in Reformed tradition, the Spirit is also not "tied to the church" (Moltmann, 1992, p. 230) which means that the church should open "itself for the wider operation of the Spirit in the world" (Moltmann, 1992, p. 231).

For Moltmann, whether you start with a social trinitarianism and a freely active Spirit in creation or a monarchical trinitarianism with the Spirit as specifically sent by the Father and the Son matters to how churches function in day-to-day life. He believes that the latter ends up as "a way of legitimating the hierarchical constitution of the church," whereas the former leads to "a community in which everyone contributes what is his or hers: it is a non-hierarchical fellowship of equals in the Holy Spirit" (Moltmann, 1992, p. 244).

Within the research project Bobby (the Minister of St. James—the squarely Open Evangelical church) demonstrated a clear commitment to a pneumatology that saw the Spirit as free. His oft-repeated phrase was that he did not have "a monopoly of the good things of God." He was very much open to the work of the Spirit in the life of the church; this included both maintaining a blurred boundary between the church and the wider community and also seeing the Spirit at work amongst the youth and children as much as the adults and seeing spontaneity as key.

Charismatic theology shares significant ground with Moltmann and Bobby. Charismatic theology democratizes church life and practices (Warrington, 2008, p. 66; Pugh, 2017, p. 50) which leads members to "expect

[4]It is worth noting at this point that the objective here is not to convince readers of the usefulness of a particular theological position—as if we should decide on what we believe based on the usefulness of each version of a doctrine—rather it is to help readers understand possible reasons for why family ministry might be found difficult in certain places and times.

to engage in participatory worship and corporate edification where every believer is viewed as charismatic and, therefore, can function as a channel for the Spirit (Romans 12:6; 1 Corinthians 12:7; Philippians 4:15; 1 Peter 4:10)" (Warrington, 2008, p. 133). This was demonstrated in the clearly Charismatic Evangelical church St. Mary's where a focus on the work of the Spirit led to an expectation of informal participation on the part of youth and children.

It is perhaps unsurprising to then hear a focus on the church and some antipathy with working with parents within Open and Charismatic Evangelical churches. For example, the Minister at St. James' read the scriptural texts as follows:

> Jesus is pretty harsh on family ties. You know, it's 'don't say to me you've got mother and brother and sisters; these are all my brothers and sisters.' No, I'm not going to use that to sort of preach against the nuclear family, but I would say actually within Scripture there is as much if not more so talking about the strength of community and the community of faith rather than it being simply an isolated nuclear family; if such a thing existed.

Henry, the Minister of the Charismatic Evangelical church was clear that he felt that the church was very much his domain of authority but that the home was not. He appeared to draw a very clear and significant line between the two to the extent that he never really thought about talking to parents as parents.[5]

Conservative Evangelical theologies of the Spirit and church contrast with the above in several significant ways. Firstly, the Spirit is far more tied to the work of the Son and to the Bible; the Spirit's main work is to illuminate the Scriptures and to point to Jesus Christ (Milne, 1998, p. 251; Ferguson, 1996, pp. 35–56; Jackman, 2006, pp. 15–25, 57–58). Additionally, instead of a focus on what God is doing 'out there' in creation, through the Spirit, there is a focus on what God does through the church and when the

[5]Rienow (2013) makes a similarly clear distinction between the church and home but does so not with the hope of church ministers avoiding the topic of family or parenting but instead with the desire to see churches understand their limited responsibility with respect to the discipleship of youth and children.

Bible is preached (Ferguson, 1996, p. 239; Jackman, 2006, pp. 109–126). It is not difficult to see how this theology of the Spirit fits more with the authority-submission structure that Ware elucidates and which fits with a family ministry model rather than the more relational-communal and altogether flatter conceptual position that fits more with the values of intergenerational ministry. Although none of the churches in the research project exhibited a Conservative Evangelical theology of the Spirit and church, the above conclusions are corroborated by the author's own experience of many different Conservative Evangelical Church of England churches.

Leadership[6]

Open Evangelicals in both the literature and the case studies are either ambivalent or actively against hierarchical authoritative leadership by a pastor-teacher as shepherd and this spills over into and is related to less of a focus on parents as accountable authoritative figures in the family.

Moltmann opposes what he calls "clericalization" in the church. From his pneumatology and doctrine of the Trinity he sees that "the church of Christ is a community of free and equal men and women who exist with one another and for one another in the charismatic diversity of their gifts and life-styles" (Moltmann, 1992, p.236). Michael Koppel appears to work from a Moltmannian framework and sees the importance of minsters learning to "get out of the way" and "cultivate a community" where people can coach each other (Koppel, 2008, p. 115).

This conceptualization of leadership was present with the minister at St. James. Bobby clearly saw himself as facilitator and coach and clearly did not like the idea of being directional in ministry. Leadership for him was about being the "shepherd that leads from the middle;" he wanted to focus on listening, not proactively suggesting which way the sheep ought to go. He explicitly expressed an antipathy toward family ministry because of the way in which it implied some forms of direction and teaching, or as he saw it, "telling people what to do" and "making them feel worse."[7] Although he had never read Jones's work on family ministry, he certainly

[6] The idea of a relationship between theology, leadership, and family ministry or intergenerational ministry has been explored in more detail by the author in Crispin, 2023b.

[7] Interestingly there were a number of people in his church that shared his wider theological outlook but nevertheless wished he would sometimes be more directive and take a clearer lead.

would not have liked the idea of "intentionally and persistently coordinating a ministry's proclamation and practices so that parents are acknowledged, trained and held accountable as primary disciple-makers in their children's lives" (Jones, 2009, p. 40).[8]

Conservative Evangelical understandings of leadership and authority are very different from the views above. For Conservative Evangelicals leadership is intrinsically and intimately bound to the preaching of the Bible, which is primarily the job of the pastor (see Kostenberger, 2014, pp. 40–54; Dever & Alexander, 2005, p. 33; Schreiner, 2014, p. 100; Ware, 2014, p. 294). Contra the Open Evangelical view, Conservative Evangelicals see leaders as shepherds who lead not from the middle but "out in front so that they can follow us to green pastures" (Dever & Alexander, 2005, p. 94). Leadership as shepherding is about other things too but essential and primary to the job is bringing back "strays" and confronting the wolves that are the false teachers (Dever & Alexander, 2005, p. 94). Leaders do not "get out of the way" to let the Spirit work but instead the Spirit works through the preaching of the Bible by the minister (David, 2014, p. 312).

Conservative Evangelicals then see a close link between the minister as shepherd of the church, and parents (and often specifically fathers) as ministers of their home, their families (Prince, 2011). There are disagreements within family ministry advocates as to how exactly the church and family relate (Jones, 2009), but in essence there is agreement about the need for parents and in particular fathers to recognize their accountability and authority as leaders of the family.

Charismatic Evangelicals sit somewhere in the middle at this point; they maintain a high view of preaching and directional leadership but their pneumatology and its democratizing effect work toward a more distributed idea of authority (Donaldson, 2011, pp. 123–26; Parkinson, 2020, pp. 96–97). As with Conservative and Open Evangelicals, this Charismatic Evangelical position on leadership is seemingly linked to its view of leadership in the home. In the Charismatic Evangelical church in the research project, Henry was clear that he wanted to affirm the place of parents in the discipleship of youth and children, but he was unsure as to how to go

[8] That is not to say that he never worked with parents and families. Indeed there were examples where he had effectively worked with parents and whole families, but he did not dwell on these instances.

about that and seemed ambivalent to the whole idea of encouraging parents in their role as leaders in the home.[9]

Scripture, Revelation, and the View of Youth and Children

All of the above fits with the varying approaches to Scripture, revelation, and the views of youth and children found in Open, Charismatic, and Conservative theologies and churches. Views will vary within each grouping but the minister, Bobby (St. James), captured at least one version of an Open Evangelical approach to Scripture. He focused on the differences within Scripture rather than the unity, its human rather than its divine origin, and a preference for the Gospels over the Epistles, especially the Pauline Epistles.

This is diametrically opposed to a Conservative Evangelical approach to Scripture and revelation which can be seen already emerging in what has been discussed above. The Bible is not divided into Jesus and Paul or seen as a work of humanity rather than God; the Bible is understood as a coherent whole (and as the Word of God through human writers) with a theology being understood as unified across the biblical canon (Dever & Alexander, 2005; Merkel & Schreiner, 2014). Revelation is primarily seen as experienced through the reading and preaching of the Bible, which is often, even normally, done by or mediated by adults.

As with leadership, Charismatic Evangelicals find themselves in some ways between Open and Conservative Evangelicals. Warrington summarized charismatic positions on the Bible as viewing it as an "encounter with the divine author" (2008, p. 189). The historical gap between reader and the text is seen as small. There is a "present-tenseness" to the Bible (Warrington, 2008, p. 190). The Bible is seen as addressing the felt needs and emotions of the contemporary reader (Warrington, 2008, p. 189). It is about "real" life in that sense. Perhaps unsurprisingly, more value is placed on the narrative sections of Scripture especially the Gospels and the book of Acts. Hermeneutically, it is the Spirit that leads the reader into the truth

[9]Clearly there are a number of other factors that might explain people's hesitancy to affirm the leadership of parents and in particular fathers in the home (for example: the concern of making single parents feel guilty, it being seen as aligned to a certain political position, or even the personal experience of the minister's own family). But theological positions on leadership appear to be a plausible contributor to the issue.

of the Bible; the Spirit inspired the Bible, so the Spirit interprets the Bible (Warrington, 2008, p. 199).

These views of Scripture (as well as the pneumatologies set out above) relate to how churches view revelation and youth and children. Within Open and Charismatics Evangelicals there is a readiness to see youth and children as people who can reveal God and not simply in the way in which they might correctly interpret the Bible but through them as beings (Nye, 2009; May, 2006; Csinos & Beckwith, 2013; Keuss, 2014; King, 2006). God's Spirit is "out there" at work and so can be seen "out there" including within youth and children.

From a Charismatic perspective, Suurmond noted "it is obvious that where there is more room for a subjective contribution, greater reference is made to the different capacities of the community" (1994, p. 24). As part of this, narrative and testimony are of upmost importance (Warrington, 2008, p. 222) such that exegesis involves, "a playful interaction between the text of the Bible and the present situation, in which the story of Scripture is interwoven with that of community" (Suurmond, 1994, p. 22). There is both a playfulness to interpreting Scripture and also a sense in which God is at work outside of the pages of the Bible.

Conclusion

The argument in this paper is that theologies and churches that draw on Open and Charismatic theology (including social trinitarianism, an active Spirit not strictly bound to the Bible and the church, a horizontal view of leadership, and a view of revelation that is comfortable with seeing youth and children as *revealers* of God) may provide fertile ground for intergenerational ministry through the resultant focus on equality, relationships, experience, and subjectivity. Family ministry on the other hand may be more naturally supported by more Conservative Evangelical theology due to its focus on the vertical aspects of relationships within the home and church. These are based on and found within Conservative Evangelical views of the Trinity, the Spirit and the Church, leadership, Scripture and revelation, and the view of youth and children. The focus on a more vertical, top-down theology is seen in Trinitarian theology where the Father sends the Son, who both then send the Spirit; in ecclesiology and leadership where the Church is led from the front by pastor-teachers, and in Scripture and revelation where the focus is on what the Bible says as understood by the mind.

Churches wishing to think more deeply about how to foster family ministry, might benefit from considering the views of their church (in terms of the denomination, the individual church as institution, as well as the range of views among church members) with respect to these areas of theology. This process should not take a lead in discerning which theology is true as theology does not automatically lead to a given approach to church life and practices. Nevertheless, a discussion around the areas of theology as discussed above could prove fruitful in examining why family ministry may be something that certain churches find harder to foster than others and to explore possible avenues for developing family ministry in every context.

References

Anthony, M. & Anthony M. (Eds.) (2011). *A theology for family ministries.* Nashville, TN: B&H Publishing.

Allen, H. C. & Ross, C. (2012). *Intergenerational Christian formation: Bringing the whole church together in ministry, community and worship*. Downers Grove, IL: IVP.

Csinos, D. M. & Beckwith, I. (2013). *Children's ministry in the way of Jesus*. Downers Grove, IL: IVP.

Crispin, G. (2023a, forthcoming). Ludicity and theology: Exploring some theological foundations of intergenerational ministry. In S. G. Ketcham (Ed.), *Intergenerate 3*. Abilene, TX: Abilene Christian University Press.

Crispin, G. (2023b, forthcoming). Leadership, family ministry and intergenerational church: Reflections from three case studies in the Church of England. *Journal of Applied Christian Leadership.*

Crispin, G. (2019). A biblical theological approach to the church home relationship. In C. Seibel (Ed.), *The Generative Church*. Eugene, OR: Wipf & Stock.

Crispin, G. (2018). Intergenerational communities and a theology of accommodation. In H.C. Allen (Ed.), *InterGenerate: How Churches Can Become More Intentionally Intergenerational in Outlook and Practice*. Abilene, TX: Abilene Christian University Press.

David, A. M. (2014). Leading the church in today's world: What it means practically to shepherd God's flock. In B. L. Merkle & T. R. Schreiner (Eds.), *Shepherding God's flock: biblical leadership in the New Testament and beyond*. Grand Rapids, MI: Kregel.

Dean, K. C. (Ed.) (2010). *OMG: A youth ministry handbook*. Nashville, TN: Abingdon Press.

Dean, K. C. (2004). *Practicing passion: Youth and the quest for a passionate church.* Grand Rapids, MI: William B. Eerdmans.

Dever, M. & Alexander, P. (2005). *The deliberate church: Building your ministry on the Gospel*. Wheaton, IL: Crossway Books.

Donaldson, W. (2011). *Word and spirit: The vital partnership in Christian leadership*. Abingdon: Bible Reading Fellowship.

Ferguson, S. B. (1996). *The Holy Spirit*. Downers Grove, IL: IVP.

Harkness, A. G. (2012). Intergenerationality: Biblical and theological foundations. *Christian Education Journal*, 9(1), 121–134.

Jackman, D. (2006). *Spirit of truth: Unlocking the Bible's teaching on the Holy Spirit*. Fearn, UK: Christian Focus.

Jones T. P. (2009). *Perspectives on family ministry: 3 views*. Nashville, TN: B&H Publishing.

Kang, S. (2011). Guest editorial introduction to the special focus: Ministry with emerging generations in a post-Christian world. *Christian Education Journal*, 8(2), 326–330.

King, M. (2006). *Presence-centered youth ministry: Guiding students into spiritual formation.* Downers Grove, IL: IVP.

Kings, G. (2003). Canal, River and Rapids: Contemporary Evangelicalism in the Church of England. *Anvil*, 20(3), 167–184.

Koppel, M. S. (2008). *Open-hearted ministry: Play as key to pastoral leadership.* Minneapolis, MN: Fortress Press.

Kostenberger, A. J. (2014). Shepherds and shepherding in the Gospels. In B. L. Merkle, & T. R. Schreiner (Eds.), *Shepherding God's flock: Biblical leadership in the New Testament and beyond.* Grand Rapids, MI: Kregel.

Keuss, J. (2014). *Blur: A new paradigm for understanding youth culture.* Grand Rapids, MI: Zondervan.

Lawson, M. S. (2011). Old Testament Teachings on the Family. In M. Anthony & M. Anthony (Eds.), *A theology for family ministries.* Nashville, TN: B&H Publishing.

Lord, A. (2003). The Pentecostal-Moltmann dialogue: Implications for mission. *Journal of Pentecostal Theology*, 11(2), 271–287.

May, S. (2006). The contemplative-reflective model. In M. J. Anthony (Ed.), *Perspectives on children's spiritual formation* (pp. 45–102). Nashville, TN: B&H Publishing.

Melick, R. Jr. (2011). New Testament teachings on the family. In M. Anthony & M. Anthony (Eds.), *A theology for family ministries* (pp. 88–105). Nashville, TN: B&H Publishing.

Milne, B. (1998). *Know the truth: A handbook of Christian belief* (2nd ed.). Leicester: IVP.

Moltmann, J. (1993). *The trinity and the kingdom: the doctrine of God.* Minneapolis, MN: Fortress Press.

Moltmann, J. (1992). *The Spirit of life: A universal affirmation.* London: SPCK.

Nye, R. (2009). *Children's spirituality: What it is and why it matters.* London: Church House Publishing.

Parkinson, I. (2020). *Understanding Christian leadership.* London: SCM Press.

Prince, D. (2011). The pastor's home as paradigm for the Church's family ministry. In R. Stinson & T. P. Jones (Eds.), *Trained in the fear of God: Family ministry in theological, historical and practical perspective.* Grand Rapids, MI: Kregel Publications.

Pugh, B. (2017). *Bold faith: A closer look at five key ideas of charismatic Christianity.* Eugene, OR: Wipf and Stock.

Schreiner, T. R. (2014). Overseeing and serving the church in the pastoral and general epistles. In B. L. Merkle & T. R. Schreiner (Eds.), *Shepherd-*

ing God's flock: Biblical leadership in the New Testament and beyond. Grand Rapids, MI: Kregel.

Stinson R. & Jones T. P. (Eds.) (2011). *Trained in the fear of God: Family Ministry in theological, historical and practical perspective*. Grand Rapids, MI: Kregel Publications.

Rienow, R. (2013). *Limited church: Unlimited Kingdom: Uniting church and family in the great commission*. Nashville, TN: Randall House Publications.

Ware, B. A. (2011). The Father, the Son and the Holy Spirit: The trinity as theological foundation for family ministry. In R. Stinson & T. P. Jones (Eds.), *Trained in the fear of God: Family ministry in theological, historical and practical perspective.* Grand Rapids, MI: Kregel Publications.

Warrington, K. (2008). *Pentecostal theology: A theology of encounter*. London: T&T Clark.

Author Biography

Gareth Crispin, Ph.D., is a lecturer in practical theology at Cliff College, United Kingdom and co-director of the college's research center for the study of mission and ministry to youth, children and families (YCF).

The Biblical Command for Home Discipleship

Graham Hale, D.Min.

Abstract: While a neglected practice for the average churchgoer, home discipleship is a practice that is called for in Scripture. God commands His people to instruct their children from His Word in the home for the purpose of reaching the lost for Christ and discipling the saved, so they grow in godliness. There are many examples of this practice found in the Bible. This article examines the more explicit biblical commands for home discipleship.

Introduction

God commands His people to instruct their children from His Word in the home. Jason Helopoulos, in *A Neglected Grace: Family Worship in the Christian Home*, explained, "Leading our families in worship is a responsibility that is given to us.... There are plenty of commands that in our homes we are to teach our children, read the Word, pray: in essence—worship" (2014, p. 30). This article will examine the biblical commands of home discipleship woven throughout Scripture, using the terms "family worship" and "home discipleship" interchangeably.

A Call for Home Discipleship in Genesis 18

God's plan from the beginning included family worship as a method to spread God's Gospel and advance His Kingdom. In Genesis 18:19, God says, "I have chosen [Abraham], that he may command his children and his household after him to keep the way of the LORD by doing righteousness and justice, so that the LORD may bring to Abraham what he has promised him" (ESV). Allen Ross commented on this passage as he wrote, "Abraham will command his household to keep the way of the Lord, to do righteousness and justice, that they might enjoy God's blessing" (1988, p. 350). Kenneth Gangel and Stephen Bramer highlighted the importance of the Lord's instruction, stating, "We dare not miss the parenting emphasis in verse 19. God had chosen Abraham so he would direct his children and his household after him to keep the way of the Lord" (2002, p. 164). Helopoulos wrote, "How would Abraham have taught his children? There was no church. Abraham would have taught them at home. Throughout the time of the patriarchs, there was no one to gather with for worship other than those in their own family" (2014, p. 31).

The command God gave to Abraham and the children of Israel extends to His people today. Joel Beeke wrote, "Those of us who are pastors, must lovingly inform the heads of families in our churches that they must command their household to worship God as Abraham did" (Beeke, 2009, p. 14).

A Call for Home Discipleship in Deuteronomy 4:9–10; 6:4–9, 20–25; & 11:18–20

Just as God commanded Abraham to teach his children to keep the way of the Lord, God spoke through Moses, calling Israel to do the same in their homes. Moses wrote Deuteronomy at the end of his life, while with God's people Israel in Moab near Jericho (Numbers 33:48–49; Deuteronomy 1:5). In Deuteronomy, the Israelites are called to remember God's great work of deliverance (Deuteronomy 5:15; 6:12; 7:18; 15:15; 24:18, 22), obey His commandments He has given them (Deuteronomy 4:23; 8:11, 18; 11:16; 12:13, 19, 30; 15:9; 16:3, 12; 24:8), and pass those teachings on to the next generation so that generations to come would know and faithfully follow the Lord (Deuteronomy 4:9–10; 6:4–9, 20–25; 11:18–20). According to C. F. Keil and F. Delitzsch,

> The Israelites were to instruct their children and descendants as to the nature, meaning, and object of the commandments of the Lord; and in reply to the inquiries of their sons, to teach them what the Lord had done for the redemption of Israel out of the bondage of Egypt, and how He had brought them into the promised land, and thus to awaken in the younger generation love to the Lord and to His commandments (Keil & Delitzsch, 1983, p. 326).

In Deuteronomy 4, Moses instructed God's people not to forget what they had seen and heard from the Lord, but to "make them known to [their] children and [their] children's children" (Deuteronomy 4:9–10). Moses placed the responsibility of home discipleship on the parents under his care. He called for them to instruct their children and grandchildren on the seriousness of sin and the importance of loving God and keeping His commands so that the mighty works of God and the commandments He has given would be remembered and maintained for generations to come. According to Jeffrey Tigay, "Every parent is to be a teacher of religion ... Deuteronomy emphasizes repeatedly that the Israelites are not to keep to themselves the experiences they had and the responsibilities they were taught: they must transmit them to their children and grandchildren" (1996, p. 46). J. A. Thompson noted, "Lest they be forgotten ... the faithful transmission of the story to the children was obligatory for Israel" (1976, p. 104).

To prepare the Israelites for their move into a land filled with pagan practices and polytheistic beliefs, Moses told them, "Hear, O Israel: The LORD our God, the LORD is one. You shall love the LORD your God with all your heart and with all your soul and with all your might. And these words that I command you today shall be on your heart. You shall teach them diligently to your children" (Deuteronomy 6:4–7, ESV). Doug McIntosh argued, "Wise parents give their children the added benefit of hearing the truth from the very beginning, so that their wayward tendencies can be brought under control early on" (2002, p. 86). Daniel Akin and Scott Pace, taught, "The Lord designed the family ... to transmit the faith from one generation to the next ... [to] preserve God's covenant people and their sacred heritage among the nations" (2017, p. 277). Parents are to instruct their children on the truths of God's person, teaching, and work so that children for generations know Him, love Him, and live for Him. J. G. McConville wrote, "[These teachings] are likewise to be passed on to the next generation, not simply by enforcing them as a law code but by making them the fabric of life and conversation" (2002, p. 142).

In Deuteronomy 6:20–25, Moses told God's people that when their children ask why they serve a different God and live counter to those around them, they are to be ready with an answer. They are to take that opportunity to instruct their children of God's great work of deliverance when He rescued them from slavery in Egypt with "signs and wonders" (Deuteronomy 6:22) and led them into the Land of Promise (Deuteronomy 6:23). They are to teach on God's great Word and on how obedience to God leads to blessing. They are to tell of the marvelous commands of God and explain how they are to live in relationship with Him as His people, fearing Him and being "careful to do all ... [that] he has commanded" (Deuteronomy. 6:25).

In Deuteronomy 11, Moses said, "You shall therefore lay up these words of mine in your heart and in your soul ... You shall teach them to your children, talking of them when you are sitting in your house, and when you are walking by the way, and when you lie down, and when you rise" (Deuteronomy 11:18–19, ESV). Eugene Merrill wrote, "Moses insisted that his words be taught to the children in such indelible ways that they would never be forgotten" (1994, 210). McIntosh argued, "No opportunity to engage in spiritual training should be lost, whether formal (talk about them) or informal (when you walk along the road), whether late (when you lie down) or early (when you get up)" (2002, p. 86). According to Keil and Delitzsch, "The commandments of God ... were to be enforced upon the children, talked of at home and by the way, in the evening on lying down and in the morning on rising up, i.e., everywhere and at all times" (1983, p. 324).

A Call for Home Discipleship in Psalm 78:1–7

While it was George Santayana who famously said, "Those who cannot remember the past are condemned to repeat it" (1998, p. 103), it was

Asaph who first communicated this idea. As Moses recounted the faithfulness of God in Deuteronomy 11, Asaph recounted "the glorious deeds of the Lord" (Psalm 78:4). In Psalm 78, he reminded the children of Israel of their missteps, (Psalm 78:8–11, 17–19, 22, 32, 36–37, 40–42, 56–58), God's judgment (Psalm 78:21, 30–31, 33–34, 59–67), and His faithfulness (Psalm 78:12–16, 20, 23–29, 38–39, 43–55, 68–72). Asaph wrote Psalm 78 so that God's people would remember and learn the lessons from history to avoid the pitfalls of those who have gone before, so that future generations would trust in the Lord and faithfully follow Him. According to H. C. Leupold, "[Asaph draws] instructive and helpful lessons from the history of God's people.... The purpose of this didactic psalm [is] to instruct the coming generation against infidelity by the clear lessons of history (vv. 1–8)" (1959, pp. 561–562).

As in the book of Deuteronomy, a key word in Psalm 78 is *remember*. Asaph reminded God's people of His great work in redemptive history and encouraged them to teach their children so that "[they would] not *forget* the works of God, but keep His commandments" (Psalm 78:7). Marvin Tate wrote, "Only by understanding the old traditions can the present generation avoid repeating the sins of the previous ones.... 'The man without memory is not able to be a faithful man'" (1990, p. 289).

Asaph told his readers that God commanded His people to teach His law to future generations so "the next generation might know them, the children yet unborn, and arise and tell them to their children so that they should set their hope in God and not forget the works of God, but keep His commandments" (Psalm 78:6–7). According to Stephen Lawson, "God commanded His people to teach their children, who in turn would tell their children (Deuteronomy 6:6–7). Each generation should entrust God's Word to the next generation" (2006, p. 15). Michael Anthony Towler noted, "This concept lays the foundation for a spiritual legacy to be established by one person that has the potential to impact dozens if not hundreds of descendants, as the Lord so blesses" (2018, p. 15). James Montgomery Boice also wrote on this legacy of faith passed down from one generation to the next: "The history of God's dealings with us must be taught to our children. We have a duty to do this because ... it is the means by which our children may come to 'put their trust in God' and 'not forget His deeds'" (1996, p. 645). According to Akin and Pace, "The result will be a godly heritage that extends through 'the next generation'" (2017, p. 278). John Philips made this exact point in his commentary on Psalm 78. Phillips explained,

> God holds parents accountable for the spiritual instruction of their children ... The father is to teach the son, the son is to teach the grandson, the grandson is to teach the great-grandson; truth is to be handed on diligently from generation to generation. God recognizes no generation gap. The gap is bridged, age after age, by the diligent teaching of the Word of God. The result? "That they might set their hope in God, and not forget the works of God, but keep His commandments." What God wants is a spiritual chain reaction. Truth my father held will become truth I hold, truth I hold will become truth my sons hold ... God has commanded this kind of instruction, and He will bless it (1988, p. 645).

A Call for Home Discipleship in Proverbs 22:6

The prayer of Psalm 78 includes a desire to see the next generation setting their hope in God. In Proverbs 22:6, one finds a similar desire; there is a hope that the next generation would go in the way of the Lord. In the verses preceding, Proverbs 22:4–5, Solomon examined both the path of the foolish and the way of the wise. He instructed his readers to take the path that honors God and leads to blessing. Solomon then called for parents to train their children in wisdom: "Train up a child in the way he should go; even when he is old he will not depart from it" (Proverbs 22:6). While this is a proverb and not a promise and cannot guarantee that a child raised in a way that honors God will never go astray, Solomon explained it is the wisest path to take toward that end (Waltke, 2005, pp. 205–206). According to Max Anders, "The word for *train* [חנך] is usually translated 'dedicate,' suggesting that we should set aside each son and daughter for God, channeling them toward holiness. Faithful, skillful training in the early years will normally produce results in adulthood" (2005, p. 127). Charles Bridges wrote,

> The hopes of at least two generations hang upon this most important rule. How can we look on a child without thoughtful anxiety? An existence is commenced for eternity.... The whole universe does not afford an object of deeper interest. It is an "arrow in the hand of a mighty man"—a most powerful instrument of good or evil, according to the direction that is given to it. Everything depends on his training. Two ways lie before him—the way in which he *would* go—headlong to ruin, and the way in which he *should* go—the pathway to heaven.... Train him as God's child—entrusted to your care, asking guidance from day to day.... Pray for him. Teach him to pray. Instruct him "from a child in the Holy Scriptures" as the sole rule of faith, and directory of conduct. Never was this training so momentous.... The alternative is not between sound principles and none; but between wholesome truth and those crude or poisonous errors, which the subtle enemy is ever ready to inject, and the corrupt heart equally prepared to receive (1968, pp. 401–403).

A Call for Home Discipleship in Isaiah 38:19

The hope of Proverbs 22:6 and the conviction of Psalm 78:4–8 can be seen in Hezekiah's proclamation found in Isaiah 38. While this hope and conviction is primarily found in just one verse, there remains a powerful reminder that fathers are to declare God's faithfulness to their children. This was not a call for only one generation of God's people. It is God's heart for the home woven throughout Scripture from one generation to the next. God's Word consistently calls parents to "devote themselves to God, diligently teach their children the commands and stories of God, repeat the teaching often, discuss the things of God in every area of life, and understand that they serve their children as representatives of God Himself" (Coley & Robinson, 2021, p. 17). Hezekiah understood this calling in Isaiah 38.

Isaiah was a prophet to the Jews in the Southern Kingdom of Jerusalem during the reign of King Hezekiah. Second Kings 18:5 describes

Hezekiah as one who "trusted in the LORD, the God of Israel, so that there was none like him among all the kings of Judah after him, nor among those who were before him." While he remained set apart from kings and devoted to the Lord during most of his earthly reign, Hezekiah became prideful. As a result, he was cursed with sickness and was told by God's prophet that he would die (Isaiah 38:1).

Hezekiah did not believe that this sentence was final and sought the Lord for rescue. God heard Hezekiah's prayer and instructed Isaiah to tell him, "Thus says the LORD, the God of David your father: I have heard your prayer; I have seen your tears. Behold, I will add fifteen years to your life" (38:5). After worshipping the Lord for delivering him from death, Hezekiah explained the reason God saved him. The first was for worship and thanksgiving. God delivered him from death to worship the Lord and thank Him for His miraculous work of salvation (38:18–19). Hezekiah prayed, "You have delivered my life from the pit of destruction ... you have cast all my sins behind your back" (38:17). According to Gary Smith, "These acts of divine intervention on behalf of Hezekiah cause the king to offer words of praise of God (38:18)" (2007, p. 650). When commenting on these verses, Martin Luther explained, "There is no greater sacrifice for a godly man than gratitude, praise, and thanksgiving for the blessings received" (1969, p. 344).

Hezekiah also explained that God forgives and restores man to a right relationship with Himself, so man makes Him known to the next generation. Hezekiah prayed to God, "The living, the living, he thanks you, as I do this day; the father makes known to the children your faithfulness" (38:19). Luther reflected on this verse and wrote, "This is taken from Psalm 78:5: 'which He commanded our fathers to teach to their children.' We publish this praise in such a way that not we but all our children publish it" (1969, p. 344). According to Smith, "Although praise was primarily directed to God, two central aspects of praise were (a) to talk about God's acts of faithfulness, His truthfulness to His promises; and (b) to tell other people (especially children in the family) of the wonderful things God has done" (2007, p. 651). John Calvin elaborated,

> Children are given to men on the express condition, that every man, by instructing his children, shall endeavor, to the utmost

> of his power, to transmit the name of God to posterity; and, therefore, the fathers of families are chiefly enjoined to be careful in this respect, that they shall diligently mention the benefits which God has bestowed on them (1996, p. 179).

A Call for Home Discipleship in Ephesians 6:4

The calling placed upon parents to train their children for godliness is not merely an Old Testament command for Jewish families. In the book of Ephesians, Paul wrote a letter addressing both Jews and Gentiles. In Ephesians 6:4, he addressed parents, fathers, in particular, as he wrote, "Fathers, do not provoke your children to anger, but bring them up in the discipline and instruction of the Lord." Frank Thielman concluded that Paul's instruction to fathers is that, "[They] should not use their authority over their children in ways that breed resentment but should instead instruct and admonish them with the teaching of Jesus" (2010, p. 403). Clinton Arnold explained,

> Fathers have the ultimate responsibility of raising their children in such a way that they will be trained in understanding the essence of the Christian faith and that they will be instructed and admonished on how to live this out.... Paul lays on the shoulder of the fathers not only the responsibility of raising their children to be decent and responsible people (which is likely assumed here as a part of the cultural expectation), but of training and instructing them in the ways of the Lord. In other words, fathers are ultimately responsible for their children's spiritual and religious education (2010, p. 418).

Whitney, in agreement with Arnold, noted, "Consistent, father-led family worship is one of the best, steadiest, and most easily measurable ways to bring up children in the Lord's 'discipline and instruction'" (Whitney, 2016, p. 25).

Conclusion

The command for parents to instruct their children in the faith remains one of the most important in Scripture. The spiritual state of future generations is dependent upon the faithfulness of the current one. God has appointed fathers and mothers to be family shepherds in their homes. The biblical commands for home discipleship and family worship are woven throughout Scripture, bringing a joyful privilege, urgent ministry, and weighty responsibility for Christian parents. Christian parents have the Word of God that they are to now "teach to their children, that the next generation might know them, the children yet unborn, and arise and tell them to their children, so that they should set their hope in God and not forget the works of God, but keep His commandments" (Psalm 78:5–7, ESV).

References

Akin, D. L., & Pace, R. S. (2017). *Pastoral theology: Theological foundations for who a pastor is and what he does*. Nashville, TN: B&H Academic.

Anders, M. (2005). *Proverbs*. Holman Old Testament Commentary. Nashville, TN: Broadman & Holman.

Arnold, C. E. (2010). *Ephesians*. Exegetical Commentary on the New Testament. Grand Rapids, MI: Zondervan.

Beeke, J. R. (2009). *Family worship*. Grand Rapids, MI: Reformation Heritage Books.

Blakley, J. (2016). Equipping Parents at Elkin Valley Baptist Church to lead family worship. D.Min. project, Southeastern Baptist Theological Seminary.

Boice, J. M. (1996). *Psalms volume 2: Psalms 42–106*. An Expositional Commentary, Volume 7. Grand Rapids, MI: Baker Books.

Bridges, C. (1968). *A commentary on Proverbs*. London: Banner of Truth Trust.

Calvin, J. (1996). *Commentary on the prophet Isaiah: Volume III*. Calvin's Commentaries, Volume 8. Grand Rapids, MI: Baker Book House.

Coley, K. & Robinson, B. (2021). *Equipping fathers to lead family worship*. Nashville, TN: Randall House.

Gangel, K. & Bramer, S. (2002). *Genesis*. Holman Old Testament Commentary. Nashville, TN: Broadman & Holman Publishers.

Helopoulos, J. (2013). *A neglected grace: Family worship in the Christian home*. Ross-shire: Christian Focus Publications.

Keil, C. F. & Delitzsch, F. (1983). *The Pentateuch*. Commentary on the Old Testament in Ten Volumes. Volume 1. Grand Rapids, MI: WM. B. Eerdmans Publishing Company.

Lawson, S. (2006). *Psalm 76–150*. Holman Old Testament Commentary, Volume 12. Nashville, TN: B&H Publishing Group.

Leupold, H. C. (1959). *Exposition of the Psalms*. Columbus, OH: The Wartburg Press.

Luther, M. (1969). *Lectures on Isaiah chapters 1–39*. Luther's Works. Saint Louis, MO: Concordia Publishing House.

McIntosh, D. (2002). *Deuteronomy*. Holman Old Testament Commentary. Nashville, TN: Broadman & Holman Publishers.

McConville, J. G (2002). *Deuteronomy*. Apollos Old Testament Commentary, Volume 5. Downers Grove, IL: InterVarsity Press.

Merrill, E. H (1994). *Deuteronomy*. The New American Commentary, Volume 4. Nashville, TN: B&H Publishing Group.

Phillips, J. (2002). *Exploring Psalms volume one: An expository commentary*. The John Phillips Commentary Series. Grand Rapids, MI: Kregel Academic & Professional Publications.

Ross, A. P. (1988). *Creation and blessing: A guide to the study and exposition of the book of Genesis*. Grand Rapids, MI: Baker Book House.

Santayana, G. (1998). *The life of reason*. Amherst, NY: Prometheus Books.

Smith, G. V. (2007). *Isaiah 1–39*. The New American Commentary. Nashville, TN: B&H Publishing Group.

Tate, M. E. (1990). *Psalms 51–100*. Word Biblical Commentary, Volume 20. Dallas, TX: Word Books, 1990.

Thielman, F. (2010). *Ephesians*. Baker Exegetical Commentary on the New Testament. Grand Rapids, MI: Baker Academic.

Thompson, J. A. (1976). *Deuteronomy: An introduction & commentary*. Tyndale Old Testament Commentary, Volume 5. Downers Grove, IL: InterVarsity Press.

Tigay, J. (1996). *Deuteronomy*. JPS Torah Commentary. Philadelphia, PA: Jewish Publication Society.

Towler, M. A. (2018). Training parents at Bethlehem Baptist Church, Louisville, Kentucky, to practice family worship. D.Min. project, The Southern Baptist Theological Seminary.

Waltke, B. (2005). *The book of Proverbs: Chapters 15–31*. The New International Commentary on the Old Testament, Volume 14. Grand Rapids, MI: W. B. Eerdmans Publishing Co.

Whitney, D. (2016). *Family worship*. Wheaton, IL: Crossway Books.

Author Biography

Graham Hale, D.Min., has served as senior pastor of Fellowship Bible Church in Jacksonville, Texas since 2010. He holds degrees from the University of Arkansas (B.A.), Mid-America Baptist Theological Seminary (M.Div.), and Southwestern Baptist Theological Seminary (D.Min.). He and his wife, Leslie, were married in May of 2003 and have three daughters.

Leveraging Family Ministry Values, Priorities, and Practices to Equip the Next Generation With a Biblical Worldview

Paul Mermilliod, Ph.D.

Abstract: Equipping the next generation with a biblical worldview is an incredibly important endeavor that should be a significant value, priority, and practice of the local church. A national research study of 518 churches representing 43 different states and Guam was conducted in 2021 through quantitative analysis to examine the values, practices, and priorities of congregations pursuing church-based family ministry. The purpose of this article is to provide a synthesis of the research study, its findings, implications, and applications for churches desiring to more strategically equip families and the next generation in pursuit of developing and deepening biblical worldview.

Introduction

"Thus says the Lord: 'Stand by the roads and look, and ask for the ancient paths, where the good way is; and walk in it, and find rest for your souls…" (Jeremiah 6:16, ESV). These significant words given by God through the prophet Jeremiah not only exist to serve God's people in ancient Israel's day, but also today. The human heart has always and will always continue to long for the "good way" and "rest for the soul" because it carries the weight of eternity within it (Ecclesiastes 3:11). Satisfaction for these longings cannot be found in saviors of the culture, which include self-actualization, autonomy, success, and prosperity. Satisfaction and joy are found in the God who is life (John 1:1–4; 10:10). It is the aim and calling of every Jesus follower to continually reorient one's life around a whole-hearted love for the God of life who is good and brings rest to the soul. One of the significant privileges and responsibilities of believers is to not only embrace this pursuit but to pass these truths on to others, including the next generation (Matthew 28:19–20; Psalm 145:4). This kind of equipping will not happen randomly or haphazardly. It requires strategy, intentionality, perseverance, and diligence.

The Need to Prioritize the Equipping of Families and the Next Generation With a Biblical Worldview Through the Local Church

The nuclear family is one of God's primary means for spiritual formation and generational faithfulness (Deuteronomy 6:1–9; Psalm 78:1–8, 127:3–5). However, in God's glorious design they are not called to pursue this responsibility and challenge on their own. Another foundational means of spiritual formation among the next generation is the people of God. The local church is called to "equip the saints for the work of the ministry" (Ephesians 4:12), which includes equipping families to make disciples at home (1 Timothy 3:4–5; Ephesians 6:4; Colossians 3:20–21; Nelson & Jones, 2011, p.16). When local churches embrace their calling to intentionally equip and work in partnership with parents and families for the sake of helping the next generation know, love, and follow Jesus Christ, gospel seeds can be planted, grow, and bear kingdom fruit (Matthew 13:1–9, 18–23). This calling and conviction of the priority of family equipping through local congregations has regained focus and momentum over the past two decades within churches and academia through the continually evolving, contemporary faith-at-home movement (Jones & Trentham, 2015, pp. 5–14). This growing movement continues to raise awareness that congregations who affirm and espouse a church-based family ministry model should prioritize the development and implementation of strategic values, practices, and priorities that equip, resource, and support the nuclear family as a locus for disciple-making (Bell, 2017, pp. 93–99).

Much work has been accomplished over the past two decades to advance the contemporary church-based family ministry movement (Anthony & Anthony, 2011; Garland, 2012; Joiner, 2009; Renfro, Shields, & Strother, 2009; Stinson & Jones, 2011). These resources discuss, explore, develop, and express theological, philosophical, and methodological foundations for contemporary family ministry models (Mermilliod, 2021). However, even with all the research and resources in the field of family ministry, there are still major hurdles facing churches and families that carry the conviction to shape the way the next generation thinks, believes, and lives in light of God's Word. These challenges include but are not limited to generational tensions, the continual advance of digital technology, the rise of anxiety-related mental health issues, a steady decline in religious affiliation and practice, a growing bias against Scripture as the source of truth, and the steady disengagement of parents in the spiritual equipping of their children (White, 2017; Twenge, 2017; Barna Group, 2018; Cooperman et al., 2015; Sierra, 2019). Even though these challenges are daunting, churches have the opportunity and calling to hold out the beauty of the gospel to the next generation and encourage them to put their hope in God. One significant action that churches and ministry leaders can take toward this end is to evaluate and assess the values, priorities, and practices that shape their ministry to families.

The Family Ministry Priority and Practice Study

In light of the biblical commands to make disciples among the next generation, the calling of the church to equip the saints for the work of ministry, and the present generational and spiritual challenges facing parents and adolescents, it is imperative that leaders within the local church prioritize the equipping of families for the sake of the gospel. However, without quantifiable baseline data, it is highly challenging to accurately and adequately evaluate the philosophical and methodological effectiveness of churches that are attempting to equip and encourage families in the pursuit of helping the next generation form a biblical worldview. While many works have been and continue to be published highlighting the importance of biblical worldview and provide theological and practical implications and applications of family ministry, a gap has remained within the precedent literature (Crawley, 2017, pp. 122–123). This gap is the lack of empirical data regarding the actual prioritization and practices of churches that affirm and espouse a church-based family ministry model (Crawley, 2017, pp. 122–123). It is for this reason that the family ministry priority and practice study was developed, distributed, and completed in 2021 (Mermilliod, 2021).

The purpose of this research study was to examine the values, practices, and priorities of congregations pursuing church-based family ministry within the Southern Baptist Convention (SBC) through a quantitative analysis. A quantitative analysis measuring practice and priority is significant because it provides empirical evidence on two levels. First, it provides actual data regarding the discipleship practices that churches are intentionally equipping and resourcing parents and families to pursue. Second, it provides an actual data comparison of the level of prioritization given to family ministry practices among churches. The scope of the study was limited in three significant ways. First, the scope of the study was limited to congregations within the Southern Baptist Convention that ascribe to a philosophy and methodology of church-based family ministry. Second, the scope was limited to the three main contemporary models of church-based family ministry, including family-based, family-equipping, and family-integrated (Jones & Stinson, 2011). Lastly, the population of the research study was limited to surveying respondents who serve in an oversight role with regard to the family ministries of their congregation (senior pastor, family pastor, student ministry director, kids ministry director, etc.).

The Primary Focus of Priority and Practice Study

The main focus of the study was to measure the values, priorities, and practices of congregations pursuing a model of church-based family ministry. Values are central in shaping behavior, providing clarity to decision-making, and facilitating shared understanding among individuals and organizations (Tichey, 1997, p. 106). Practice is described as the actions, often housed within ministry services and programs, as the pursuit of congregations to "strengthen families through discipling them to live biblical principles in their daily life together" (Garland, 2012, p. 552).

Priority is the elevation and emphasis of specific actions and efforts (Garland, 2012, pp. 533–535).

In order to empirically ascertain family ministry values, practices, and priorities, intentional questions were asked of church leaders within the study. First, in order to assess family ministry values, respondents were asked to select family ministry practices that they considered to be significant values within their ministry to families. Second, in order to assess prioritization, respondents were asked to provide a personal assessment of the annual percentage of financial expenditures (ministry dollars) and ministerial activities (time spent doing ministry) that were allotted for each family ministry value selected. The findings from these criteria allowed the researcher to have a quantifiable means by which to measure stated values of churches pursuing a family ministry strategy in comparison and contrast to their actual family ministry priorities and practices.

Survey Design Overview

The research for the analysis of family ministry priority and practice within the SBC was completed in three stages. First, the researcher labored to find precedent studies in the field of youth and family ministry that could serve as a foundation for the development of the instrumentation for his study. Upon much investigation, two significant studies were found that provided a direction and framework for valid instrumentation that could be utilized within a study of church-based family ministry (Broyles, 2009; Crawley, 2017). These two studies provided thirteen essential family ministry practices along with the means to measure values, financial expenditures, and ministerial activities of family ministry leaders across the country (Mermilliod, 2021). The thirteen practices that were evaluated were regular times of family prayer, regular devotions and faith talks at home, equipping parents for home-based discipleship, regular family worship times, equipping and support for parents in child-rearing, marriage enrichment, families adopting spiritual orphans, families serving together on mission, church leadership casting vision for family ministry, premarital preparation, equipping and support for families in crisis, intergenerational corporate worship, and church leadership kept accountable in their relationships.

The second stage was to take the thirteen essential family ministry practices from Crawley's research and the instrumentation design from Broyles' research and utilize them to develop survey instrumentation. The third and final stage was to conduct the research and analyze the results. The survey itself was designed electronically by the researcher, hosted by Survey Monkey, and approved for distribution by the Research and Ethics Committee chair at Southeastern Baptist Theological Seminary (SEBTS).

Online Questionnaire

The online survey had four main sections. First, the questionnaire asked participants to provide demographic information related to their congregation and to themselves. This demographic data included church location by zip code and setting, average worship attendance, the current age of the respondent, length of tenure at current church, length of tenure in vocational ministry, formal ministry training, and model of contemporary family ministry. Second, respondents were asked to select family ministry practices that are significant values within their congregation's ministry to families. Third, respondents were asked to provide a personal assessment of the annual percentage of financial expenditures allocated for each family ministry practice they selected. Finally, respondents were asked to provide a personal assessment of the annual percentage of ministerial activities (time spent doing family ministry) allocated for each family ministry practice they selected.

The Findings of the Family Ministry Priority and Practice Study and Their Potential Impact on Equipping Toward a Biblical Worldview

The survey development, random sampling of the population, and the distribution of the online questionnaire were accomplished by the researcher in partnership with LifeWay Research and SEBTS. There were 5,000 churches selected within the SBC through random sampling to participate in the survey. Of those churches, approximately 10% participated in the study. The 518 churches that participated in the study were from 43 different states and Guam. Their location within their community ranged from rural to suburban to urban.

Participants in the study ranged in age from 21 years old to 83 years old, ranged in tenure at their current church from less than one year to 50 years, and ranged in tenure in vocational ministry from less than one year to 62 years. Churches in the study varied in average attendance from less than ten people to 4,500. Ministry leaders who participated in the research study had a range in backgrounds in formal ministry training, which included a graduate degree in ministry to families, a graduate degree in religion, an undergraduate degree in ministry to families, an undergraduate degree in religion, and other/not applicable. There were 457 churches that participated in the study that ascribed to the family-based, family-equipping, or family-integrated model of contemporary family ministry.

Significant Values of Churches Pursuing Family Ministry

The findings from the research revealed that the top four family ministry practices deemed "significant values" across all survey responses were "encouraging and providing regular intergenerational corporate worship" (88% of responses), "providing premarital preparation" (71% of responses), "equipping and resourcing for devotions and faith talks at home" (62% of responses), and "equipping and resourcing families to serve together on mission" (56% of responses). Restated, intergenerational worship, premarital counseling, devotions and faith talks, and missional living occurred on more than half of all responses. These four values could be defined as the most prioritized stated practices of family ministry for congregations ascribing to a church-based model of family ministry within the SBC.

A middle tier of family ministry practices deemed as "significant values" included "equipping and support for families in crisis" (47% of responses), "equipping and resourcing parents for home-based discipleship" (47% of responses), "providing equipping and resources for marriage enrichment" (45% of responses), "equipping and resourcing for regular family worship times" (45% of responses), "equipping and support for parents in child-rearing" (44% of responses), and "equipping and resourcing for regular times of family prayer" (44% of responses). These six values all occurred in a very close range of response between 44%–47% of the total data received.

The least selected family ministry practices deemed as "significant values" included "providing accountability for church leadership in their own family relationships" (40% of responses), "providing vision casting for family ministry by the church leadership" (38% of responses), and "equipping and resourcing families to adopt spiritual orphans" (17% of responses). It is important to note that leadership accountability and vision casting both occurred on one-third of all participants' survey data; however, adoption of spiritual orphans was included on less than one-fifth of all responses.

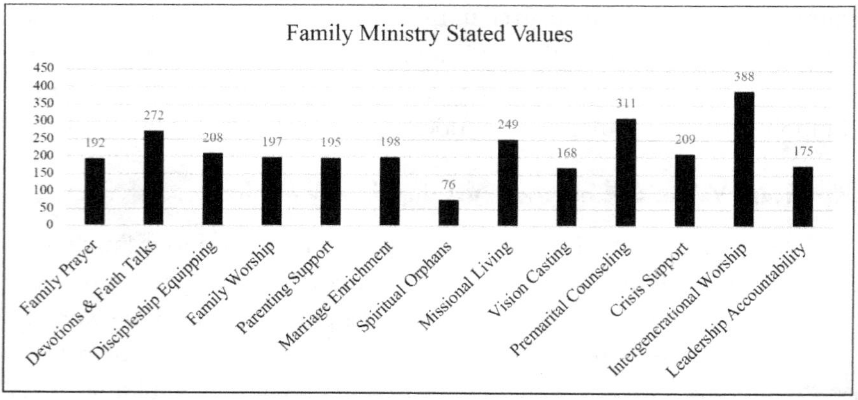

The findings from the research study also speak to the actual prioritization of the family ministry practices of respondents. In order to quantifiably measure priority, stated family ministry "significant values" were measured against the actual annual financial expenditures and ministerial activities allotted to said values. The following charts highlight the percentage of money and time allotted for each family ministry practice.

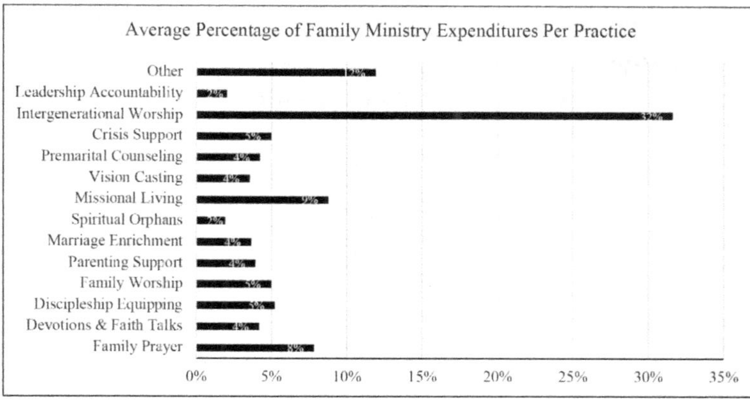

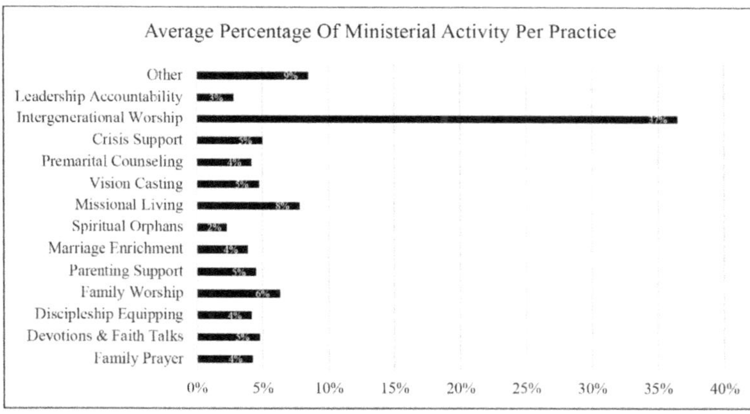

Research Implications and Applications for Equipping the Next Generation With a Biblical Worldview

Numerous implications and applications can be drawn from the family ministry priority and practice study. The following observations have been limited to those that most directly impact churches desiring to better equip and partner with families in helping the next generation develop a biblical worldview. The following section describes seven highlights from the study that could be leveraged as practical implications and applications for church leaders desiring to equip families and the next generation with a biblical worldview.

The Need for Critical Ministry Evaluation in the Pursuit of Equipping the Next Generation With a Biblical Worldview

One of the significant benefits of the family ministry priority and practice study was that it filled a void in the precedent literature. While much research and resource development has been accomplished in the field of family ministry, there had yet to be a national study that surveyed the actual values, priorities, and practices of congregations pursuing a model of church-based family ministry. This reality highlights the need for theologians and practitioners to not only address the theology, philosophy, and methodology of family ministry, but also to address and emphasize the importance of evaluation and assessment in ministry to families. The family ministry priority and practice survey can be utilized as a practical tool for evaluation that church leaders can leverage as they develop a strategy for equipping families and the next generation with a biblical worldview.

The Importance of Family Ministry Values

One of the findings from the family ministry priority and practice study was that stated values do have a direct impact on family ministry practice. While this might seem intuitive, the study quantifiably verified that there is a statistically significant relationship between stated values and programmatic priorities of congregations pursuing a church-based family ministry model. Statistically, this means that churches that identify and highlight the importance of equipping parents to help their children develop a biblical worldview are more likely to allocate funding, time, and attention to this end than those that do not.

The Need to Assess and Close the Priority and Practice Gap

As previously stated, one of the conclusions from the research project is that there is a statistically significant relationship between stated values and programmatic priorities in family ministry practice. However, there is also a disconnect in stated values and actual behaviors among family ministry practices deemed as "significant values." Many of the top "significant values" provided by family ministry leaders did not proportionately reflect the same value in their annual spending and allotment of time. This finding speaks to a potential disparity between the priority of family ministry values and the actual practice of said values among family ministry leaders. One implication for churches is to work to close the gap between stated values and actual behaviors in their ministry to families. Closing the gap could occur through a reassessment of a church's family ministry values and practices. Closing the gap could also involve a reallocation of annual financial expenditures and ministerial activities toward specific family ministry practices.

Addressing the Lack of Priority and Practice in Family Discipleship

One of the significant findings from the research study that directly relates to the topic of churches intentionally equipping families and the next generation with a biblical worldview is the data related to *discipleship equipping* and *devotion and faith talks*. The total financial expenditures and ministerial activities given to these two practices combined for an average of less than ten percent of the annual investment of church leaders surveyed. Restated, on average, church leaders prioritized less than ten percent of their annual budget and time to equipping parents to disciple their children at home. This could be a major factor leading to a deficit in the next generation's understanding of a biblical worldview. One way that churches and leaders can be more intentional to help the next generation grow in their understanding of Scripture and how it shapes the way one thinks, believes, and lives is to equip parents to consistently make disciples at home. Two examples of practical resources that churches can utilize to help them in this pursuit are D6 Curriculum (*D6 EveryDay Curriculum*, n.d.) and the Family Discipleship Plan (*The Family Discipleship Plan*, n.d.).

Maximizing the Opportunity to Leverage Intergenerational Worship to Equip the Next Generation With a Biblical Worldview

Another finding derived from the family ministry priority and practice study was that "encouraging and providing regular intergenerational corporate worship" ranked as the most valued essential family ministry practice of congregations pursuing a church-based family ministry model. However, just because this is the most significant family ministry priority and practice of churches surveyed does not necessarily mean that this practice is being fully leveraged as a means to equip parents and the next generation with a biblical worldview. One application from the findings of this study would be for family leaders to work with the pastors and elders who are responsible for the weekly worship gathering to address specific ways to intentionally help the congregation grow in their development of a biblical worldview. A strategically aligned effort to align family ministry equipping and the weekend preaching around the specific aims related to worldview could be a potent combination for not only the spiritual growth of the whole congregation, but also the adolescents.

Not Forgetting Spiritual Orphans in the Pursuit of Helping the Next Generation Develop a Biblical Worldview

Another conclusion derived from the research is the need for churches to prioritize the practice of more strategically "equipping and resourcing families to adopt spiritual orphans." This essential family ministry practice was by far the lowest stated value and received the least amount of allocation of annual financial expenditures and ministerial activities per practice. Conversely, it is interesting to note that "equipping and resourcing families to serve together on mission" was one of the top four stated values, financial expenditures, and ministerial activities. There appears to be a disconnect between these practices; it is likely that many churches aren't considering spiritual orphans in their strategy to equip the next generation, but there is an opportunity for churches to reach a large percentage of children and teens that have little to no gospel influence.

The Absence of Strategic Leadership in Family Ministry

A final conclusion worth noting in relation to the pursuit of equipping families and the next generation with a biblical worldview is related to the issue of strategic leadership. The findings demonstrated that the stated value and programmatic priority given to the two practices that specifically addressed leadership were among the lowest scores across the study. These practices are "providing accountability for church leadership in their own family relationships" and "providing vision casting for family ministry by the church leadership." Scripture has much to say regarding pastors and leaders being examples to the church (1 Peter 5:1–4; 1Timothy 3:1–7; Titus 1:5–9). Local churches that ascribe to a church-based family ministry model would be wise to assess the value they place on vision casting and leader accountability in the development of their plan to help equip families and the next generation with a biblical worldview.

Conclusion

In Psalm 78, Asaph paints a picture of faithful discipleship of the next generation. He wrote, "We will not hide them from our children, but tell to the coming generation the glorious deeds of the Lord, and his might, and the wonders that he has done.… So that they should set their hope in God and not forget the works of God, but keep his commandments" (Psalm 78:4, 7, ESV). The calling to help the next generation, "set their hope in God" is simultaneously a weighty responsibility and a joyous opportunity.

While church-based family ministry is complex, challenging, and ever-changing, Great Commission advancement to the next generation through the family is achievable through the work of the Holy Spirit. In his work *Evangelism in the Early Church*, Michael Green describes what God can do through only a few individuals who commit to following Jesus with their whole heart. He wrote:

> It was a small group of eleven men whom Jesus commissioned to carry on his work and bring the gospel to the whole world. They were not distinguished; they were not well educated; they had no influential backers. If they had stopped to weigh up the probabilities of succeeding in their mission, even granted their conviction that Jesus was alive and that his Spirit went with them to equip them for their task, their hearts must surely have sunk, so heavily were the odds weighted against them to succeed. And yet they did (Green, 2003, p. 221).

As the church labors to make Jesus known among the next generation, the prayer of this study is the same prayer that apostle Paul articulated in his letter to the church at Ephesus, "Now to Him who is able to do far more abundantly than all that we can ask or think, according to the power at work within us, to Him be glory in the church and in Christ Jesus throughout all generations, forever and ever, Amen" (Ephesians 3:20–21).

References

Anthony, M. J. and Anthony, M. (2011). *A theology for family ministry*. Nashville, TN: B&H Publishing, Kindle Edition.

Barna Group and Impact 360 Institute (2018). *Gen Z: The culture, beliefs and motivations shaping the next generation*. Ventura, CA: Barna Group.

Barna Group and Impact 360 Institute (2021). *Gen Z volume 2: Caring for young souls and cultivating resilience*. Ventura, CA: Barna Group.

Bell, P. (2017). A practical strategy for partnering with the family. *D6 Family Ministry Journal, 2*, 93–99.

Broyles, D. R. (2009). An analysis of SBC youth ministry programmatic values investigated through financial expenditures and ministerial activities. Doctoral dissertation, The Southern Baptist Theological Seminary.

Cooperman, A., Smith, G., & Ritchey, K. (2015). America's changing religious landscape: Christians decline sharply as share of population; Unaffiliated and other faiths continue to grow. Pew Research. https://www.pewforum.org/2015/05/12/americas-changing-religious-landscape/.

Crawley, S. D. (2017). Moving towards definitional consensus in contemporary family ministry: A Delphi study. Ph.D. dissertation. Retrieved from https://searchproquest-com.ezproxy.sebts.edu/docview/2029172783?accountid=130758.

D6 EveryDay Curriculum. (n.d.). https://d6family.com/d6curriculum.

The Family Discipleship Plan. (n.d.). https://familydiscipleshipplan.org.

Garland, D. R. (2012). *Family ministry: A comprehensive guide.* 2nd ed. Downers Grove, IL: IVP Academic.

Green, M. (2003). *Evangelism in the early Church.* Revised Edition. Grand Rapids, MI: Eerdmans.

Joiner, R. (2009). *Think orange.* Colorado Springs, CO: David C. Cook Publishing.

Jones, T. P., & Trentham, J. D. (2015). *Practical family ministry: A collection of ideas for your church.* Nashville, TN: Randall House.

Jones, T. P., & Stinson, R. (2011). Family Ministry Models. In M. J. Anthony & M. Anthony (Ed.), *A theology for family ministry* (pp. 4488–5356, Kindle Edition). Nashville, TN: B&H Publishing.

Nelson, B., & Jones, T.P. (2011). The problem with family ministry. In R. Stinson & T. P. Jones (Ed.), *Trained in the fear of God: Family ministry in theological, historical, and practical perspective* (pp. 13–29). Grand Rapids, MI: Kregel Academic.

Mermilliod, E. P. (2021). A synthesis of academic research related to church-based family ministry. *CEJ* , 406–419.

Mermilliod, E. P. (2021). Strategic church-based family ministry: An analysis of family ministry priority and practice within the Southern Baptist Convention. Ph.D. dissertation, *The Southeastern Baptist Theological Seminary.*

Renfro, P., Shields, B., & Strother, J. (2009). *Perspectives on family ministry: Three views.* Edited by Jones, T.P. Nashville, TN: B&H Publishing Group.

Sierra, L. K. (2019). Secular students' perceptions of Christian rhetoric: A phenomenological study," Ed.D. thesis. Retrieved from https://www.proquest.com/pqdthss/docview/2317613517/BC6A96BF04AF4EFBPQ/1?accountid=130758.

Tichey, N. M. (1997). *The leadership engine: How winning companies build leaders at every level.* New York, NY: HarperCollins.

Twenge, J. M. (2017). *iGen: Why today's super-connected kids are growing up less rebellious, more tolerant, less happy-and completely unprepared for adulthood.* New York, NY: Atria Books.

Twenge, J. M. (2017). *Meet generation Z: Understanding and reaching the new post-Christian world.* Grand Rapids, MI: Baker Books.

White, J. E. (2017). *Meet generation Z: Understanding and reaching the new post-Christian world.* Grand Rapids, MI: Baker Books.

Author Biography

Paul Mermilliod, Ph.D., is a lead pastor of Tri-Cities Baptist Church in Johnson City, Tennessee. Paul has his Ph.D. in Applied Theology from Southeastern Baptist Theological Seminary, is a published author, and a chief creator and editor of the Family Discipleship Plan. Paul is married to Katie, and they have four children: Jack, Evelyn, Camden, and Tripp.

Discipleship in a Post-Truth Culture

R. Allen Jackson, Ph.D.

Abstract: We live in a culture that is characterized by a definition of *truth* based more on emotion than on evidence. We study a Bible that says that Truth is a person and not a concept and that we can know the Truth and be freed as a result. In the collision of opposite worldviews, biblical discipleship is allowing our story to be absorbed into the grand story that is life as a Jesus-follower.

Introduction

The year 2016 was a turning point year, a defining year for America. Kobe Bryant played his last NBA game. Peyton Manning retired from the NFL. The Chicago Cubs won the World Series for the first time since 1908, allegedly breaking the curse brought upon them for trading Babe Ruth to the Yankees. For the first time in more than five decades, a United States cruise ship set sail for Cuba. The news was full of shootings, including police shootings, several mass shootings, and even one shooting at an elementary school in South Carolina (CNN, 2017).

Politically, the year was a tsunami. President Barack Obama nominated Merrick Garland for the Supreme Court, but his nomination stalled in Congress. Hillary Clinton was the first woman to lead the presidential ticket of a major political party and her opponent was celebrity Donald Trump. Both candidates had issues in their past and present which made the presidential campaign a distasteful one to watch. Clinton was heavily favored and as late as October, a credible news agency put her odds of winning the electoral college at 95% (Reuters, 2016). Trump's victory in

November was shocking to most, but his election coincided with another first-place finish that was less celebrated, but which was potentially as telling as the presidential election.

The Oxford English Dictionary's 2016 word of the year was "post-truth." It was placed in the 2016 edition of the dictionary alongside 1,200 new words and phrases. Post-truth is defined as "relating to or denoting circumstances in which objective facts are less influential in shaping public opinion than appeals to emotion and personal belief" (Oxford, n.d.).

This casual, yet stunning addition to the dictionary both reflected and refracted. It reflected the direction that culture had already headed, putting definition to an observable trend. It refracted the light of historical understanding of truth, giving it an entirely different meaning altogether. In the years that followed the "year of post-truth," America became more partisan, more divided, more committed than ever to truth based on emotion and little else.

When Jesus said that "the truth will set you free" (John 8:32), He both affirmed the overt meaning and implied something much deeper. On the surface, parents, teachers, coaches, and youth pastors tell students that a lie requires more lies to cover/explain the original lie. Common experience (mine) confirms that the lies keep building up until they crash in the revelation of falsehood. Historical wisdom suggests that the liar will experience guilt and when truth is finally revealed, guilt is relieved and relationships are restored. True, but that is not what the verse is about.

The deeper meaning here is that truth is not a concept, a worldview, or a dictionary definition, but a person. The way of Jesus is the way of truth, and in John 8:32, Jesus referred to Himself as 'truth' and taught that to 'know the truth' is to follow Him in complete faith. This is the truth that brings freedom. Freedom is eternal life, abundant life, supported life, community life, and compassionate life, all embodied in the teachings of Jesus. Discipleship, therefore, is based on, defined by, and rooted in the 2 Timothy 2:2 premise that the way of Jesus is passed on from generation to generation of believers.

To know the truth is to know Jesus. Truth is a person. If truth is a person, it changes the dialog about discipleship.

When we were young, truth was an adjective. Math answers were true (correct) or not. Truth was what the history books said was true—appropriately questioned in contemporary culture. We took true/false quizzes, judging declarative statements, and "true" indicated the rightness of a statement. Truth was objective, knowable, and discoverable.

Yet today, the notion of truth being objective has given way to truth based on emotion. In American culture, we have migrated from religion based on superstition, to modernity, to post-modernity, and to post-truth. Truth as objective reality (outside of self) has increasingly been perceived as unknowable or even non-existent. The defining characteristic of post-modernity was a rejection of absolute truth. As George Knight observed, "The basic issue of conflict between Christianity and postmodernism is that the first is founded upon revealed absolutes, while the second denies both the concept of absolutes and the possibility of revelation" (2006, p. 100).

Any current claim to truth is met with skepticism at best or even the accusation that any declaration of truth is a bid for power. Post modernity gave us "personal truths," a euphemism for subjective desires that shift with time, circumstance, and partisan politics–mostly based on feelings.

Jesus, did not place feelings ahead of truth, much less did He consider truth to be irrelevant or unknowable. Quite the contrary, He promised His disciples that they would know the truth, and that the truth would set them free (John 8:32). He Himself claimed to be the way, the truth, and the life (John 14:6). He even confronted "post-truth" in His own day, in the form of Pontius Pilate's sarcastic question, "What is truth?" (John 18:38).

The premise of this paper is that truth, grounded in the person of God, is knowable, objective, and absolute. God is God and we are not and He is who He says He is, not who we might wish Him to be. He has revealed Truth in the person of His Son whether we recognize it or not. Such a declaration is the heart of discipleship and generally puts disciples at odds with popular culture.

From Superstition to Post-Truth

I became interested in the role of truth in American culture while I was teaching youth culture classes in seminary. I was fascinated with the link between sociology and youth ministry in the church. Every culture has basic elements of family, economy, communication, law, and religion. In terms of religion, my students studied the commonalities across cultures, including the natural inclination to believe that there has to be something greater than what is seen. I talked in class about the migration from superstition to modernism to postmodernism to post-truth culture.

Superstition, embraced from early Western civilization to ancient Greece—and perhaps returning in the middle ages—believed in the supernatural, but held that God (or gods) punished persons who did evil things and rewarded persons who did good things. In the modern era of Western civilization, generally from the Enlightenment through the fall of Communism in the former Soviet Union, human reason replaced supernaturalism. Particularly in the 20th century, modernism emerged as a secular ideology with a bent to science, invention, and humanism. Modernism gave way to post-modernism in the latter half of the 20th century, a well-documented phenomenon that was particularly common in academia.

In postmodernism there are no absolutes; it rests on the assumption of existentialism and is a reaction to modernity. However, postmodernism is not a philosophy or a worldview in that it does not necessarily propose to be for anything. There are no principles or beliefs postmodern thinkers have agreed upon, so defining postmodern worldview is like nailing Jell-O to a wall. Glenn Sunshine in his article for the Colson Center commented,

> Arguably, the roots of much postmodern thought can be traced back to the German Enlightenment philosopher Immanuel Kant. Kant's metaphysics began with the argument that we cannot know things as they are in themselves, but only as they appear to us. In other words, our ability to perceive sets the limits on our knowledge of the world, which of necessity is always mediated to us by our senses. Objective reality is thus inaccessible to us; all our knowledge is always and inevitably subjective (Sunshine, 2019, para. 14).

In a precursor to the migration to post-truth culture, Sunshine went on to observe that a byproduct of postmodernism was a growing support for cultural relativism, the idea that we should not judge people in other cultures by our own standards since all cultures are equally valid in their own context. One of the few things cultural relativists recognize as objectively wrong morally is any attempt to impose our values, norms, religion, or anything else on other cultures (Sunshine, 2019).

The Impact of Post-Truth Culture on the Next Generation

Authors Miloš Broćić and Andrew Miles (2021) took the data set from the National Study of Youth and Religion (NSYR) and asked a different question, that of the impact of higher education on attitudes related to moral relativism, concern for others, and concern for social order. Ironically, the implied effect on a college student is that moral relativism is decreased under the constant diet of liberal moral absolutes in university environments. In other words, the morality of college students is less open to diverse points of view and more attached to rigid—and liberal—positions in politics, social justice, and religion (Broćić & Miles, 2021, p. 873). The university culture that seems to inculcate liberal values in such a manner that postmodern moral relativism is decreased and is replaced by an absolutism regarding liberal political positions on moral, social, and religious issues indicates a migration to a post-truth culture.

Moral relativism (postmodernity) and cultural relativism (we judge other cultures on the basis of our own) as university curriculum is not new. In the past decade, concern has been expressed that liberal morality curriculum is indoctrinating much younger students with regard to sexuality, gender dysphoria, and critical theory (Copland, 2021).

While it is essential and right to relate historical events and movements accurately and instructively, children have more recently been taught that truth is a subjective construct, that truth is "my truth" or "your truth" and not necessarily based on objective reality. The objective reality is not always pleasant to consider—American history in elementary through high school has traditionally been weighted to stories of American exceptionalism. Postmodernism caused a swing in the opposite direction, with children (in some instances) now being taught that certain "progressive" viewpoints are absolute and correct. These viewpoints include ideas such as, "one is either oppressed or oppressor," "your body is yours to do with as you wish," and "you don't have to remain the gender of your birth." The same moral relativism is applied to sexual orientation, gender identity, euthanasia, and a host of other ethical issues being taught to the next generation (Jackson, n.d.).

The next generation is not only exposed to such teachings through education and curriculum but encounter the same sort of messages in media today. A recent movie brought this to light. In his review of a 2022 Disney animated movie, Brett McCracken took issue with the agenda advanced. He noted the normalized lesbian lifestyle of the hero's partner:

> Progressives act like it's absurd and irrational for parents to be concerned about this queer "representation" in a Disney kids movie. Chris Evans, who takes over the voice of Lightyear from Tim Allen, has said that those who find the gay plot problematic are "idiots" who are "afraid and unaware" and will "die off like dinosaurs." Essentially admitting that becoming "woke" is the primary value at play in Lightyear, Evans said in the same interview that "what makes us good" is "social advancement as we wake up ... constant social awakening" (McCracken, 2022, para. 8).

McCracken continued,

> Is this really what makes us good? Are parents and conservatives bigoted and delusional for wanting their kids to be morally formed in history, tradition, old Christian wisdom, and ideals that haven't changed—as opposed to rapidly changing mores and "constant social awakening"? Is virtue reliable when it's pitched as something so fluid, changing dramatically from decade to decade? (McCracken, 2022, para. 9).

We have heard terms like "alternative facts," "fake news," and "felt truth," all the while observing that more and more people are ready to ignore facts, eschew evidence and willingly accept obvious lies. It would include "spin" or "selective memory" or omission of parts of a story that do not endorse a narrative we wish to embrace. In very simple terms, "the facts don't really matter, only my feelings do." As authors David Knights and Torkild Thanem wrote, "Since facts and expert knowledge are frequently dismissed as 'fake news' or drowned out in a deluge of 'alternative facts,' simply offering more data and facts may not work against politicians and people who show resistance to facts that conflict with their prejudices or feelings" (Knights & Torkild, 2019, para. 6).

In many ways, it is a natural outgrowth of relativism. Instead of absolute truth, there are only "personal truths"—subjective desires that shift with time, circumstance, or point of view. A claim that truth is universal, objective, or exclusive (especially in the case of Christianity) is increasingly met with scorn in the public arena or even labeled as oppressive.

The feelings or preferences of an individual have been elevated to the place of highest authority. As Brian Haynes wrote, "The tragedy, unless something changes, is that today's children will live a warped, individualistic, self-serving form of Christianity. They'll make decisions based on feelings rather than truth" (Haynes, 2009, p. 29). Perhaps saddest of all is that to merely disagree with another's "personal truth" is considered to be an act of hatred. The church is not immune. Even within the church, we have disagreed over many issues and in our world today, the result is often speech or behavior that is anything but Christ-honoring (Jackson, n.d.).

The tension between biblical discipleship and a post-truth culture is rooted in the embracing of an idea or point of view on the basis of emotion/feelings rather than on the basis of objective facts/truth. Jesus did not place feelings ahead of truth. In His famous conversation with Pilate in John 18:38, He confronted the world's definition of truth. He told the disciples that they could and would know the truth, and that the truth would set them free (John 8:32). He claimed to be the way, the truth, and the life (John 14:6). Truth was a person, a person who lived, breathed, taught, was crucified, buried, and rose from the dead. He, Truth, is knowable, objective, and absolute.

In the World and Not of It: Discipleship in Post-Truth Culture

"Be in the world, but not of the world" is a phrase that has almost become cliché in Christian circles. Like its cousin, "love the sinner, hate the sin," it has been diluted by the casual reference to walking the fine line between the pleasure of the world and the demands of discipleship. For the purposes of this paper, however, the phrase accurately describes the tension. It would be tempting to determine that the world is too far gone and not worth our participation in it. Rod Dreher (2017) suggested such a possibility in his book, *The Benedict Option: a Strategy for Christians in a Post-Christian Nation*. Jesus didn't seem to advocate reclusive cloistering for His disciples. He said to "go into all the world" to make disciples. He told the disciples that they were to be in the world (John 16:33) and He prayed that they would not be taken out of the world, but that they would be protected in it (John 17:14–16). In John 15:19, He told them He had "chosen them out of the world" yet His emphasis in the verse is on how the world would treat them.

If He intended for disciples to become reclusive and hide from the culture in Christian communes, He probably would have modeled that with His own followers. It was His interaction with the various other cultures (Roman, Jewish, Greek) that eventually led to His crucifixion. Jesus was light to the darkness and called His disciples to follow this example. The apostle Paul understood this responsibility to be salt and light in the world (Romans 12:2; Ephesians 4:22–24; 1 Thessalonians 4:1). As light in the world, Christians follow the example of Jesus while leading others to know Him as well.

Discipleship is a call to follow Jesus, imitate Jesus, learn from the teachings of Jesus, and encourage others to become followers as well. Jesus said that if anyone would become His follower, it involved denial, not promotion of self (Luke 9:23). The relationship between disciple maker and disciple is not one of narcissistic manipulation, regardless of the prevailing tension in our culture.

The common denominator in all of these characteristics of a post-truth culture is that they disconnect humans from humans. An idea is much easier to oppose than a person. Jesus didn't allow a person to become an idea or a point of view. He called Nicodemus, a Pharisee to explore what it meant to be born again. He invited Matthew, a despised tax collector to become a disciple. He shared water and eternal life with a Samaritan woman. He looked Pilate in the eye and insisted that truth was a relationship: "Everyone on the side of truth listens to me" (John 18:37, NIV). The restoration of the link between truth and humanity is necessary because in its simplest form, behavior that is post-truth is a power grab, "a preferred tactic of narcissistic and aggressive personalities bent on doing whatever it takes to gain and maintain a position of advantage over others" (Keane, 2018, para. 32).

Discipleship is relationship. Discipleship is a process of replication, multiplication, and perseverance. Within the confines of culture, Jesus told His first-century disciples to replicate and by extension, that is what He tells disciples today. Whether pre-Christian or post-truth, the practice of discipleship remains the same.

In my book *Disciple* (2014), I suggested that the five basic components of discipleship are Scripture memory, hermeneutics (understanding the story or narrative of the Bible), ability to articulate one's testimony, confidence in sharing the gospel with another person, and demonstrating concern regarding gospel-centered social justice. I still believe the list to be useful, but with some post-truth culture caveats. I propose that as followers of Jesus, we prioritize our relationships as a response to the post-truth culture.

Prioritize the Relationship With God Through His Word

I have done numerous Bible reading plans through the years and I sometimes find myself reading to get through the plan. However, when I read Psalm 8, I am reminded that as I read Scripture, I am seeking God. I am not seeking solutions to "back up with verses" or searching for a "great passage for a sermon." I am seeking God. I am seeking the One whose name is majestic in all the earth, the One who put all things here, and the One who is above the heavens and the earth.

Discipleship in a post-truth culture focuses on a relationship with God through His Word. Those aiming to disciple the next generation will tirelessly lead them to delight in the Word of God and know Him more. We seek the Lord through His Word, for, "We want more of Him because He is not just good to us; most important, He is good for us" (English, 2020, p. 37).

To know God through His Word means to memorize Scripture, meditate on it, linger on a story or a passage or a verse. Donald Whitney championed the spiritual discipline of memorizing Scripture when he wrote, "The goal is to memorize the Word of God so that it can transform our minds and our lives" (Whitney, 1991, p. 47). A disciple who is in the world and not of it pays attention to the God of Scripture without emotional defensiveness and without a sense of hopelessness for the social order or for the culture. Memorizing Scripture should be a priority for disciples because it places value on words that are God's words. It places value on truth in a post-truth culture.

Prioritize the "Big Picture" of God as Told in Scripture

Google Earth has given us the ability to look at our neighborhood from outer space. Well, nearly outer space. To zoom in from the globe to my driveway is pretty cool and it sort of gives me a sense that my driveway is connected to a street that is connected to other streets that are connected to highways. To zoom in on my house alone eliminates the perspective that streets and sidewalks connect us to other people. In a similar way, we also miss the connection with the bigger picture of Scripture if we only pick certain verses or stories for instruction. In academics, we call this "hermeneutics," which means to understand the story or narrative of the Bible.

In J.T. English's book, *Deep Discipleship*, he advocated for a discipleship approach that includes "a class on the story of the Bible" while "equipping [disciples] on how to read the Bible" (English, 2020, p. 106). It remains imperative for disciples today to know how to read the story of the Bible and how to understand the big picture of Scripture.

To grasp the grand story arc of the Bible is to embrace it as a metanarrative. Ruth is connected to Romans and Esther is connected to Ephesians and Genesis is connected to Galatians by the purposeful nature of God. To zoom in without zooming back out is to miss the point of God's nature, of the beauty of His creation, and of the plan of redemption through Jesus' birth, life, death, resurrection, and promised return. The metanarrative of the Bible is the complete Gospel. When we reduce or selectively comprehend the Scripture, we limit the wisdom God gives us through it (McCracken, 2021).

Prioritize the Relationship of Your Story With the Grand Story

I got to serve on jury duty once. During the one jury trial where I got to serve, I heard lawyers object over and over by shouting "hearsay" during the testimony of one witness or another. If someone did not personally experience or observe, or hear a particular action (in this case, a crime), then their words are inadmissible in court. Only first-person accounts are allowed.

In many ways, our story—our testimony—is like being on the witness stand in the court of a post-truth culture. What did you observe? What have you heard? What do you know to be true from your own personal experience? The ability to articulate one's testimony is critical in discipleship. A disciple is compelled to share his or her story because it is great news. When we share our testimony, we are sharing with others about the transformation that Jesus has brought to our lives.

We see a desire to share such testimonies woven throughout Scripture. In Psalm 71, the writer proclaims, "My mouth will tell of your righteous acts, of your deeds of salvation all the day" (Psalm 71:15, ESV). In another Psalm we read, "Come and hear, all you who fear God, and I will tell what he has done for my soul" (Psalm 66:16, ESV). First Peter 3:15 reads, "Always be ready to give a defense to anyone who asks you for a reason for the hope that is in you" (HCSB). Similarly, there is a heart throughout Scripture to share such testimonies specifically to the next generation (Exodus 13:14; Joshua 4:6–7; Psalm 78:4–7; Psalm 145:4).

Testimonies are told in relationship. The majority of Americans today do not trust media, but one might trust a journalist that they know personally. Some people might have a bad impression about Christianity and Christians, but they might listen to a personal story from a personal friend. All of us are more receptive to authentic, personal stories of faith than to lectures about ideas.

If you are new to the idea of sharing your faith story, start with a simple outline that I learned in college. Talk about what your life was like before you began to follow Jesus. Talk about your understanding of sin and how it separated you from God. Tell how you realized that Jesus would forgive you of your sin and how you invited Him into your life. Tell what difference it has made to you to be a follower of Jesus. This outline is similar to Paul's approach to sharing his testimony in Galatians 1:13–24. A simple and authentic testimony is a refreshing change in a culture of embellishment and provocative narratives.

Prioritize Inviting Other People to Follow Jesus

While discipleship in a post-truth culture will find Christians sharing their stories of faith, Christians must go beyond simply sharing their testimony and they must prioritize inviting other people to follow Jesus. Sometimes Christians may tell their stories of faith, how Jesus changed their lives, how it is better to follow Him in a mixed-up world, and they can be excited, convincing, and sincere. Quite possibly, the person to whom they are speaking is ready to make a faith commitment. However out of fear of rejection, lack of confidence in sharing the gospel with another person, or even worrying about being perceived as intolerant, the Christian may thank the person for their time and walk away without inviting them to follow Jesus.

Some may be offended that I would even suggest that the post-truth culture has succeeded in silencing many Christians. It is worth remembering, however, that it is vital to invite someone else into a Jesus story of their own. As English wrote, "To be a disciple of Jesus is to make other disciples of Jesus" (2020, p. 163).

Prioritize Actions That Reflect a Concern for the Marginalized

Maybe one of the most uncomfortable subjects for disciples in a post-truth world is that of social concern for the marginalized and underserved. Gospel-centric social justice is commanded throughout the Bible as a way to extend God's plan and purpose to the nations—even those who do not embrace His covenant (Russ, n.d.). One of Jesus' most famous parables was The Good Samaritan (Luke 10:25–37), a story that told of a Jewish man who was mugged and robbed yet was aided by another man who was of an ethnic group generally at odds with the Jews. Jesus' point was that caring for physical needs is a way to lend authenticity to meeting spiritual needs.

Trevin Wax pointed out the urgency of sharing our faith in "a world bent on believing lies" (Wax, 2022, para. 16). He articulated what is at stake:

> We bear witness to the beauty of the imago Dei in every human being, no matter their ethnicity, age, country of origin, or social status.

> We bear witness to the sacredness of all human life, including growing life enclosed in a woman's womb.
>
> We bear witness to the goodness of the created order, opposing the wanton destruction of God's good earth just as we stand against philosophies and ideologies that do harm to male and female bodies under the guise of "inclusivity" or "freedom."
>
> We bear witness to the truth when we call political parties to account for their pretensions and falsehoods, no matter how noble their causes might be.
>
> We bear witness to the truth when we submit our scholarship to the beauty and authority of God as the Author of Scripture, even when it'd be easy to wriggle out of the Bible's difficult commands and become, in the words of Kierkegaard, "kissing Judases"—followers who betray Christ with an interpretation.
>
> We bear witness to the truth when we seek to sort truth from error—refraining from slandering brothers and sisters in Christ and from spreading falsehoods like fire through our lips in conversation or our fingers online (Wax, 2022, para. 17–22).

Eric Russ summarized the necessity for social justice to be an outflow of biblical discipleship:

> The Bible is clear that the church is to advocate for the poor and the marginalized in the world, caring for their needs and pursuing justice on their behalf. We are not to neglect spiritual needs for social ones, nor social needs for those that are spiritual. The two areas of need are not in opposition. On the contrary, Christ demonstrated care for the whole person, body and spirit. As His followers, we must demonstrate the same, not allowing bad theology, laziness, and poor excuses to keep us from addressing the social needs of our communities (Russ, n.d., last para.).

Conclusion

We live in a world that is messed up. Inflation is up, truth is down. And yet God gave us a couple of very simple, very accessible instructions as to how to live "in the world, but not of the world," even when that world has rejected Truth for a worldview of post-truth. Jesus declared that He was the truth, the way, and the life (John 14:6) and that no one could come to God except through following Him. Paul wrote in Ephesians 4:15 that Christ-followers are to "speak the truth in love."

Disciples living in a post-truth world can find a balance of speaking and loving. Speaking honestly is not a reflection of not loving. When we are informed about the culture, weigh the urgency of others coming to Christ, and vocalize a testimony that is authentic, we speak truth in love. Jesus never hesitated to criticize false teachers whether they were in the church or in the culture. Notice Paul did not say, "shout the truth in self-righteous piety" but to speak the truth in love. Speaking implies a face-to-face conversation that is rooted in relationship, mutual respect, and a desire for discipleship.

James, the brother of Jesus said it well: "My dear brothers and sisters, take note of this: Everyone should be quick to listen, slow to speak and slow to become angry, because human anger does not produce the righteousness that God desires (James 1:19–20, NIV). Being "quick to listen" means that we hear even those with whom we disagree. Without interruption, we wait for them to finish before diving in with our opinion. Being "slow to speak" means that we think before we speak, planning our response in a way that speaks truth in love–and speaks to the authenticity of our discipleship in a world that is inauthentic at best. We control our words and don't blurt out everything that comes into our heads. Jesus said, "The mouth speaks what the heart is full of" (Matthew 12:34, NIV), and "the things that come out of a person's mouth come from the heart, and these defile them (Matthew 15:18, NIV).

Jesus calls Christians to be salt, light, and a city on a hill. In the midst of darkness and confusion, the light of Christ and the truth of the Word of God shines brightly. As one author wrote,

> The Oxford Dictionaries may have made "post-truth" the word of the year in 2016, but there's no such thing as a "post-truth world" or a "post-truth society." There are only those who ignore the truth and those who seek to bring themselves in line with it. And so, more than ever, we must pray for the grace to

> bear witness to the truth of Christ with the love of Christ, with faithful hope in an outcome secured by the Savior whose heel crushed the father of lies (Wax, 2022, last para.).

We can rail at the culture, or we can influence it. Wise disciples don't have to be the smartest people in the room. They have learned that more wisdom can be gained by listening, observing, and not rushing to judgment, all the while being "confident in this very thing—that He who began this good work will complete it in Christ Jesus (Philippians 1:6).

References

Allen, J. (2014). *Disciple*. Birmingham: YM360 Publishing.

Allen, J. (n.d.). From cultural relativism to a post-truth culture. In J. Denton (Ed.), *Ancient Text/Modern World: Teaching Our Ancient Text to a Modern Student*. Unpublished manuscript.

Broćić, M., & Miles, A. (2021). College and the "culture war": Assessing higher education's influence on moral attitudes. *American Sociological Review, 86*(5), 856–895. Retrieved from https://doi.org/10.1177/00031224211041094.

CNN (2017). 2016 in review: Fast facts. Retrieved from https://www.cnn.com/2016/11/14/world/2016-in-review-fast-facts/index.html.

Copland, J. (2021). How to regulate critical race theory in schools: A primer and model legislation. Policy paper from Manhattan Institute. Retrieved from https://files.eric.ed.gov/fulltext/ED615229.pdf.

Dreher, R. (2017). *The Benedict option: A strategy for Christians in a post-Christian nation*. New York, NY: Penguin Random House.

English, J. T. (2020). *Deep discipleship: How the Church can make whole disciples of Jesus*. Nashville, TN: B&H Publishing.

Haynes, B. (2009). *Shift: What it takes to finally reach families today*. Loveland, Colorado: Group.

Keane, J. (2018). Post-truth politics and why the antidote isn't simply 'fact-checking' and truth. *The Conversation*. Retrieved from https://theconversation.com/post-truth-politics-and-why-the-antidote-isnt-simply-fact-checking-and-truth-87364.

Knight, G. R. (2006). *Philosophy & education: An introduction in Christian perspective.* Berrien Springs, Michigan: Andrews University Press.

Knights, D. & Thanem, T. (2019). Fake news: emotions and experiences, not more data, could be the antidote. *The Conversation*. Retrieved from https://theconversation.com/fake-news-emotions-and-experiences-not-more-data-could-be-the-antidote-123496.

Kroet, C. (2017). 'Post-truth' enters Oxford English Dictionary. Retrieved from https://www.politico.eu/article/post-truth-enters-oxford-english-dictionary.

McCracken, B. (2022). Speeding in opposite directions: 'Lightyear' and 'Maverick'. *The Gospel Coalition*. Retrieved from https://www.thegospelcoalition.org/article/lightyear-top-gun-maverick.

McCracken, B. (2021). *The wisdom pyramid: Feeding your soul in a post-truth world*. Wheaton, IL: Crossway

Oxford Learners Dictionary (n.d.). Retrieved from https://www.oxfordlearnersdictionaries.com/us/definition/english/post-truth.

Reuters (2016). Clinton heavily favored to win electoral college. Retrieved from https://www.reuters.com/article/us-usa-election-poll/clinton-heavily-favored-to-win-electoral-college-poll

Russ, E. (n.d.). Social concern: Caring for the poor and marginalized. *Discipleship Defined.* Retrieved from http://www.discipleshipdefined.com/resources/social-concern-%E2%80%93-caring-poor-and-marginalized.

Smith, C. (Director). (n.d.). National Study of Youth & Religion. *University of Notre Dame*. Retrieved from https://youthandreligion.nd.edu.

Sunshine, G. (2019). The rise of postmodernism: Emerging worldviews 3. *Breakpoint Colson Center*. Retrieved from https://www.breakpoint.org/the-rise-of-postmodernism-emerging-worldviews-3.

Wax, T. (2022). There's no such thing as a post-truth world. *The Gospel Coalition.* Retrieved from https://www.thegospelcoalition.org/blogs/trevin-wax/no-post-truth-world.

Whitney, D. S. (1991). *Spiritual disciplines for the Christian life*. Colorado Springs, CO: NavPress.

Author Biography

R. Allen Jackson, Ph.D., is a husband, father, grandfather, professor, and pastor. He currently serves as the senior pastor at the Dunwoody Baptist Church of Atlanta, Georgia as well as part-time faculty at the New Orleans Baptist Theological Seminary (where he served full time for 22 years). He is the author of numerous articles, books, chapters in books, curriculum, and sermons.

Reimagining Biblical Worldview Education

Rebecca Aniol, Ph.D.

Abstract: Since the 1970s, Christian textbook companies have committed to biblical worldview—information aligned with biblical presuppositions. However, theological and historical scholarship over the last twenty years has emphasized that the term *worldview* more rightly relates to heart-orientation through the imagination, specifically linguistic imagery, not simply philosophical presuppositions. Thus, the evaluation of whether Christian textbooks present biblical worldview should be based not merely on the degree to which their informational content aligns with biblical presuppositions but on the degree to which that information orients the heart through linguistic imagery. The article concludes with three levels of imaginative language for evaluating textbooks.

Introduction

Christian educators have long recognized the need for a biblical worldview in Christian education. Conservative evangelical educators have championed biblical worldview education as seen in Frank Gaebelein's 1954 "call … for a wholly Christian world view on the part of our education" (Gaebelein, 2009), Kenneth Gangel's 1978 "demand for the development of a Christian world and life view" in Christian education (Gangel, 1995), Arthur Holmes's 1985 book entirely dedicated to *The Making of a Christian Mind: A Christian World View and the Academic Enterprise* (Homes, 1985), and Douglas Wilson's 1991 insistence that "true Christian education requires that a biblical worldview be successfully passed on to the students" (Wilson, 1991). As evangelicals began opening Christian day schools in the 1960s at a rapid rate in the wake of surging secularization in American public schools, evangelical educators soon realized that secular textbooks hindered the efforts of Christian education. "Biblical worldview" textbooks became the new standard in evangelical education.

Christian textbook publishing companies, first appearing in the 1970s and early 1980s, each committed to presenting Christian students with a biblical worldview of the various academic subjects. Abeka told Christian educators that they could "count on high academics and a biblical worldview" (Abeka, n.d.). BJU Press made its mission to "produce Christian educational materials with academic excellence from a biblical worldview" (BJU Press, n.d.). Christian Liberty Press is dedicated to "finding, evaluating, and producing curriculum materials that are rooted in the Word of God and express a biblical worldview" (Christian Liberty Press, n.d.). Veritas Press promised "innovative new technology with a classical education, all from a Christian worldview" (Veritas Press, n.d.). Memoria Press offered texts "developed from the perspective of a Christian worldview" (Memoria Press, n.d.). Master Books sought to "ensure that a biblical worldview is integral to all of [their] curriculum" (Master Books, n.d.) and Simply Charlotte Mason committed to "support a Christian worldview" in their curricular materials (Simply Charlotte Mason, n.d.).

In 1976, at the same time Christian publishers were releasing these new biblical worldview textbooks, James Sire defined the term worldview in a handbook on the concept, one of the first of its kind. He called worldview "a set of presuppositions" (Sire, 1976). In Sire's 1985 forward to *The Making of the Christian Mind*, he added, "the integration of academic work and the Christian faith involves the *analysis* of world views.... With *world-view analysis* we have a valuable academic tool" (Holmes, 1985, p. 8). Christian educators, in keeping with Sire's accepted definition, presented worldview as a way to *think* or reason from the lens of Scripture—as philosophical presuppositions based on Scripture that answer life's deepest questions such as: What is prime reality? What is a human being? Why is it possible to know anything at all? (Sire, 2009, pp. 22–23; Overman, 2006, p. 8; Moreland & Craig, 2003, pp. 1–7, 17).

In more recent days, however, this early definition has come under attack. The preoccupation with "worldview analysis" and "worldview thinking" led some educators to advocate the abandonment of the term (Smith,

2011, pp. 15–24; Crouch, 2008, pp. 60–64). Critics like James K. A. Smith argue that this conception of worldview "stems from [a] stunted anthropology" (Smith, 2011, p. 16). Andy Crouch wrote that Christians cannot "think [them]selves into new ways of behaving" (Crouch, 2008, p. 64). In an interview over educational methodology, Peter Leithart went so far as to say that he is "ready to delete 'worldview' from the Christian vocabulary" (Phillips, 2014).

Additionally, in 2002, David Naugle wrote a seminal study entitled *Worldview: The History of a Concept* (2002). His book instigated a mentality shift across the field regarding the definition of worldview. Naugle inextricably tied the term worldview to the heart as conceived in Scripture. He claimed that "when 'worldview' is reinterpreted in light of the doctrine of the heart, not only is its true source located, but it becomes a richer concept than its philosophical counterpart, being more than just a reference to an abstract thesis about reality" (Naugle, 2002, p. 270). He emphasized that the heart comprises the "central, defining element of the human person ... comprehensive in its operations as the seat of the intellectual ... affective ... volitional ... and religious life of a human being" (Naugle, 2002, p. 268).[1]

In response to Naugle's study and other scholarly criticism of the term, James Sire, a longtime leader in the worldview discussion, rewrote his definition of worldview. Rather than calling worldview "a set of presuppositions," he now defined worldview as "a fundamental orientation of the heart" (Sire, 2014, p. 141). He further asserts, based on his enlightened understanding of worldview, that he considers "Charles Taylor's notion of *social imaginary* as a replacement term for *worldview*" (Sire, 2014, p. 14). Taylor defined social imaginaries as "ways people imagine their social existence" and noted that the social imaginary is "often not expressed in theoretical terms, but is carried in images, stories, and legends," as "shared by large

[1]Naugle points the reader to various Scripture passages for each of these categories. Intellectual: Proverbs 2:10a; Proverbs 14:33; Daniel 10:12; Romans 1:21; Hebrews 4:12. Affective: Exodus 4:14; Psalm 13:2; Jeremiah 15:16; Matthew 22:37–39; John 14:1, 27; 2 Corinthians 2:4. Volitional: Judges 5:15; 1 Chronicles 29:18 Proverbs 16:1; Romans 1:21; 2 Corinthians 9:7; Hebrews 4:12. Religious: Deuteronomy 6:5; 2 Chronicles 16:9; Ezekiel 6:9; Ezekiel 14:3; Acts 8:21; Romans 2:29; 2 Corinthians 3:3. Craig Troxel similarly argues that the scriptural reference to the heart implies "a 'hidden control-center.' Everything we think, desire, choose, and live out is generated from this one 'controlling source' and is governed from this one point." See Troxel, *With All Your Heart: Orienting Your Mind, Desires, and Will Toward Christ* (Wheaton: Crossway, 2020), 19.

groups of people," and as "mak[ing] possible common practices" (Taylor, 2004, p. 23). Kevin Vanhoozer explains that "Taylor's 'social imaginary' is another name for the metaphors by which we live" or, in other words, "indwelling stories ... the storied understanding that is implicit in our everyday practices" (Vanhoozer, 2016, p. 37).

Restated, social imaginaries are the stories that tell how a group of people imagine the world—their worldviews. Worldviews are not mere intellectual beliefs but are images, metaphors, and stories that people hold dear in their hearts—mind, will, and affections in union.

In light of the fundamental change in the definition of worldview, how should Christian educators present a biblical worldview in textbooks? In other words—as worldview has been more closely examined and more carefully defined in evangelical scholarship over the last fifty years since the birth of modern Christian textbooks—how do Christian textbooks go about orienting the heart? More specifically, what role should "imaginaries"—images, metaphors, and stories—play in Christian textbooks that aim for a robust biblical worldview presentation? Can textbooks that aim to present a biblical worldview retain the same linguistic form that they had in the era when worldview was approached as presuppositions and analysis?

If worldview is an orientation of the heart through linguistic imagery, then the evaluation of whether or not Christian textbooks actually present a biblical worldview needs to be based not merely on the degree to which its informational content aligns with biblical presuppositions but on the degree to which that information orients the heart through linguistic imagery.

The Imagination

If social imaginary is a "replacement term for worldview," as Sire asserts (Sire, 2014, p. 14), then what exactly are the implications of this equation? Charles Taylor clarifies that he uses the term *imaginary* because he is speaking of "something much broader and deeper than the intellectual" (Taylor, 2002, p. 106). He is describing not just how people *think* about their social existence but rather how they *imagine* it—"how they fit together with others" (Taylor, 2002, p. 106). Therefore, if worldview equals social imaginary, then worldview is something "much broader and deeper than the intellectual." Worldview relies on the imagination.

Taylor's explanation brings insight into exactly what the imagination does in forming worldview—it allows people to see how they "fit together" (a synthetic understanding of identity) and ultimately creates "common practices."[2] Indeed, an examination of the scriptural, historical, theological, and linguistic understanding of the imagination shows that the imagination primarily interprets and integrates. One might say that the imagination puts together the puzzle pieces to form a picture of the world by which people live.

The Imagination in Scriptural Understanding

Alison Searle and Mark Leeds both point out that the original languages of Scripture do not have a word for *imagination*, and thus to derive a definition for the imagination from Scripture proves difficult. Nevertheless, both scholars have undertaken the task of defining the imagination from Scripture with careful effort. Searle examined the various words translated as "imagination" in English versions of the Bible and looked at their meanings to find patterns of use. The most predominant word translated as "imagination" in the Old Testament, *yetser*, literally means "form," "framework," or "frame of mind" (Searle, 2009, p. 32).[3] Searle significantly pointed out that the biblical words for heart (*leb*, *lebab*, and *kardia*) are also often translated as "imagination." The words for heart, she noted, encompass all the other meanings for imagination put together (2009, pp. 33–35). In light of this, Scripture seems to indicate that a biblical understanding of imagination is inextricably related to the heart, the mind, and the concepts of form and framework. Searle concluded that

[2] James K. A. Smith calls these common practices "cultural liturgies," by which he means the rituals and everyday practices of groups of people which shape their loves. Smith relates cultural liturgies to worship and to education as shaping worshipers. See James K. A. Smith, *Desiring the Kingdom: Worship, Worldview, and Cultural Formation* (Grand Rapids: Baker Academic, 2009); James K. A. Smith, *Imagining the Kingdom: How Worship Works* (Grand Rapids: Baker Academic, 2013); James K. A. Smith, *Awaiting the King: Reforming Public Theology* (Grand Rapids: Baker Academic, 2017).

[3] For example, Psalm 103:14 translates this term as "frame," stating, "For He Himself knows our frame [*yetser*]." In Isaiah 26:3 the term translated "mind" is this same word: "You keep him in perfect peace whose mind [*yetser*] is stayed on you" (ESV).

the imagination, biblically, should be defined as "the eyes of [the] heart" (2009, pp. 33–40). Mark Leeds likewise argued that "the two main biblical ideas that are connected to the imagination are the heart and the mind" (Leeds, 2005, p. 20).

While these observations on the use of the imagination in Scripture are indeed helpful, the imaginative forms that constitute Scripture itself offer additional insight on the biblical view of the imagination. Scripture is composed neither of lists of laws and facts nor as a systematic theology textbook. The inspired and inerrant Word of God comes to man as a piece of imaginative literature. Leland Ryken explained that "a touchstone that allows readers to gauge whether a text is literary is the degree to which they can see universal human experience in it"—not only what *happened* but what *happens*—universals, not simply particulars. By this definition, he estimated that over eighty percent of the Bible is literature (Ryken, 1990, pp. 9–10). He argued that "the preponderance of literary writing in the Bible shows that God trusted literature as a medium for conveying truth" (1990, p. 10). He further stated that over one-third of the Bible is poetry proper and that "beyond these predominantly poetic parts of the Bible, figurative language appears throughout the Bible" (1990, pp. 259–260).

Thus, the Bible—in its stories, its poetry, its drama, its visionary literature, and its vast amounts of linguistic imagery—is a book that engages the imagination. The Bible is a work of imaginative literature. Ryken concluded that "the stories of the Bible thus combine the two tendencies of narrative that have most appealed to the human race. They are factually realistic and romantically marvelous. They bring together two impulses that the human race is always trying to join—reason and imagination" (Ryken, 1990, p. 139).

The Imagination in Historical Understanding

In addition to the importance of the imagination to Scripture, both in combining the innermost parts of man and in providing the supreme examples of imaginative form, various thinkers through the centuries have discussed the nature of the imagination. Leeds helpfully surveys and summarizes definitions of the imagination in the overall history of ideas. He traced the concept of the imagination as far back as Plato, noting that for Plato the imagination is the "ability of the mind to picture things[,] which is informed by both the senses and judgment. It is a faculty that is capable of both reproduction and production. This means that it can be helpful in remembering the past, living in the present, and hypothesizing about the future. As it does these things it is capable of producing emotion" (Leeds, 2005, p. 8).[4] Augustine took Plato's conception of the imagination one step further, suggesting that all these functions of the imagination are for the ultimate purpose of spiritual maturity or sanctification (Leeds, 2005, p. 12). Spinoza first connected the imagination with language, and Kant first contributed the idea that the imagination functions synthetically to create paradigms. Leeds noted that "this notion tied to Kant's understanding of synthesis suggests that the imagination may play a passive and continual role in one's perception of all existence and thus may be relevant in the discussions surrounding the development of worldviews" (2005, p. 17).

Thus, philosophers in history understood the imagination to have primarily an interpretive and integrative function. All of these ideas contribute to the current evangelical discussion of the definition of imagination and its importance for the development of worldview.

The Imagination in Theological Understanding

Kevin Vanhoozer argued that the Christian imagination forms the foundation for the whole system of Christian doctrine and how that plays out in everyday life. He wrote, "faith is the enduring ability to imagine God, the world, and ourselves in the light of the biblical story of salvation" (2016, p. 25). Vanhoozer identified several primary aspects of the imagination. He wrote, first, that the imagination is "a faculty for making or discovering connections and meaningful forms. Analytic reason takes things apart; the synthetic imagination puts things together … the way parts 'belong to' a whole." Also, he built upon the work of Alison Searle to call the imagination the "eyes of the heart" (Eph. 1:18). Like the heart, which he noted is the "locus of volition, emotion, and belief or unbelief (Psalm

[4]Unlike Leeds, I would say, in keeping with Platonic understanding and vocabulary, that the imagination is capable of producing affections and passions, not "emotion."

14:1)," the imagination also "engages the mind, will, and emotions alike" in integrative function. He additionally emphasized the combination of synthetic coherence and the eyes of the heart to say that the imagination is "a way of looking at things together, a *seeing as*" (2016, p. 26). Thus, he concluded that "only the imagination—the ability to grasp meaningful patterns or conceive unified wholes out of apparently unrelated elements—enables us to 'see' God and the kingdom of God at work in the world" (2016, pp. 24–27).

Garrett Green described the imagination as that which "makes present through images what is inaccessible to direct experience" (1998, p. 62).[5] The imagination eliminates this *inaccessibility*; it makes them real for the reader by carrying the reader on the wave of metaphor—the vehicle of the imagination. Green further argued that the imagination is paradigmatic. In other words, it considers the past, present, and future to make connections and show a pattern or example. The imagination finds universal and cultural patterns to create norms. Green pointed out that "realistic imagination … relies entirely on paradigms to gain access to the 'transcendent,' taken here in its literal sense as the 'world beyond'—any aspect of reality outside the 'mesocosm' of familiar experience" (1998, p. 69). He further explained that "imagination *is* the taking of paradigms to explore the patterns of the larger world" (1998, p. 69).

Modern evangelical literary scholars and theologians use this scriptural, historic, and theological understanding of the imagination as interpretive and integrative to explain worldview formation. Ryken sees the imagination as a vehicle to worldview, calling the imagination the "maker of worlds" and saying that "'worldmaking' is a prime activity of the artistic imagination" (1989, p. 98). He further clarifies that the ways the imagination works "give us a heightened sense of reality.... Works of music, literature, and art are a window or lens through which we perceive reality" (1989, pp. 110, 113). He explicitly explains that "it is a fallacy to think that one's worldview consists only of ideas.... A person may say that God created the world, but if his mind is filled with images of evolutionary

[5]Inaccessible realities made accessible through the imagination, explains Green, can be inaccessible *temporally* (including memory, history, and the future), *spatially* (including non-proximal objects, microcosmic realities such as subatomic structures, and macrocosmic realities such as cosmology), and *logically* (such as metaphysical beings).

processes, he will start to think like an evolutionist.... The imagination is a leading ingredient in the way people view reality" (1990, p. 393).

Gene Edward Veith and Matthew Ristuccia similarly argued that "the imagination plays an important role in integrating our ideas and our feelings, the outer world and our inmost selves" (2014, p. 18). They further discussed the imagination as the "mind's eye," asserting that "the imagination often provides the subject matter and the impetus for our reasoning, our feelings, and our choices" (2014, p. 14). They observed that, in integrative function, "a Christian imagination is key to the formation of a Christian worldview" (2014, p. 109).

Thus, in a fully-orbed understanding of the imagination based on Scripture, history, and theology, the imagination may be defined as the eyes of the heart, that which makes worlds (or paradigms) by interpreting patterns and integrating them in the heart into a whole. Restated, imagination puts together the puzzle pieces to form a picture of the world by which people live.

The Imagination in Linguistic Understanding

One other aspect of the imagination, however, deserves further attention. Vanhoozer, in arriving at his definition of imagination, explained that the imagination works primarily through *words*, not pictures. He noted that "in the beginning of the imagination is the *word*, not the image. Christians of all people should be able to affirm this (Vanhoozer, 2016, p. 26)." He reminds readers that God created the world with words, including humans made in God's *image*, and that Scripture itself comes to the human race in words. Veith and Ristuccia (2014) likewise concluded that the imagination communicates primarily through language. They wrote, "language is precisely what stimulates and feeds the imagination" (p. 112). They further clarified that visual images such as pictures and screen images are "the production of *someone else's* [emphasis added] imagination. When we read a story ... our own internal imagination is at work" (2014, p. 112). Thus, if the imagination works primarily through words, it necessarily works in the way that words communicate—through metaphor.[6]

The word metaphor comes from the Greek *metapherein*, which literally means "to carry across, to transfer" (Ryken, 1990, p. 264). In simplest terms, metaphor connects something abstract to something concrete—something in the physical world of human experience. Ryken explained that "metaphor secures an effect on one level and then asks the readers to transfer that meaning to another level.... The very definition of metaphor suggests such a transfer" (1982, p. 11). Metaphor is the language of association or relationship—identifying one thing in terms of another. Ryken again clarified that "correspondence is the essential ingredient of a metaphor" (1990, p. 263). Correspondence then requires interpretation, the work of the imagination.

Metaphors occur in all the genres of Scripture, not only in the Psalms and other poetry sections.[7] To be clear, to say that the Bible uses metaphorical language is not to suggest that Scripture is less than inerrant, propositional truth. Scripture is fact. However, what these conservative theologians suggest is that the Bible is *more* than a mere collection of propositional facts. Ryken stated that "a literary approach takes the images of the Bible seriously as something that embodies and communicates truth" (1993, p. 15). Vanhoozer asserted that Scripture is "more than divine data"

[6]The term metaphor here refers to the correspondence nature of language, not the more specific definition of a metaphor as a literary device of implied comparison between two terms, though that is included in the broader definition. It is outside the scope of this article to delve into the metaphorical nature of language, though it is touched on in the next section about the change in language in modernity. For a fuller explanation, see Paul Riccoeur, *The Rule of Metaphor: Multidisciplinary Studies of the Creation of Meaning in Language,* trans. Robert Czerny (Toronto: University of Toronto Press, 1981), 6, 199, 212–13, 231; Eva Feder Kittay, *Metaphor: Its Cognitive Force and Linguistic Structure* (New York: Clarendon, 1987); David J. Bryant, *Faith and the Play of Imagination: On the Role of Imagination in Religion* (Macon: Mercer University Press, 1989), 92–103; Warren W. Wiersbe, *Developing a Christian Imagination: An Interpretive Anthology* (Wheaton: Victor, 1995), 21–26; George Lakoff and Mark Johnson, *Metaphors We Live By* (Chicago: University of Chicago Press, 2003); Northrop Frye, *The Education Imagination* (Bloomington: Indiana University Press, 1964); Northrop Frye, "The Expanding World of Metaphor," *Journal of the American Academy of Religion 53,* no. 4 (December 1985): 585–98.

[7]Jesus Christ is a Vine, a Door, the Bread of Life, a Light, a Shepherd, a Lamb, and a Bridegroom. God is a Father, a Warrior, a Potter, a Rock, and a Sun and Shield. The church is a bride, a household, a body, and a temple. Christians are salt and light, branches, soldiers, athletes, farmers, priests, and adopted sons. The parables of Christ are extended metaphors. The entire book of Hosea is an extended metaphor.

(2005, p. 5). He argued that "without some propositional core, the church would lose its *raison d'etre*, leaving only programs and potlucks. At the same time, to reduce the truth of Scripture to a set of propositions is unnecessarily reductionist" (2005, pp. 100–101). He contended that "biblical authority is a matter not only of revealed information (i.e., propositions) but also of larger-scale patterns of information processing (i.e., poetics)" (2011, p. 251). He further stated that "literary forms are less containers than lenses; they do not simply deliver information but are rather means of information processing that organize the data in meaningful patterns.... One cannot reduce a form to its informative content, then, without losing the very pattern of information processing" (2011, p. 256). Vanhoozer explained that "among figures of speech, metaphors are the prime exhibit of the imagination's verbal dimension" (2016, p. 28) calling metaphors "a fundamental scheme by which people conceptualize the world and their own activities" (2016, p. 28).

Warren Wiersbe asked, "What is there about metaphorical language that gives it so much power?" and answered that "metaphors affect *the whole personality*" (1995, p. 24). He clarified that "live" (vivid, living) metaphors are what "powerfully 'connect' the mind and heart of the hearers so that they want to do something in response to what they learn" (1995, p. 25). This idea of "live" (or living) metaphorical language—that language which connects the mind, will, and affections—plays an important role in how the imagination works to form worldview. David I. Smith and Susan Felch similarly reflected that metaphorical language offers "orienting images that might consciously or unconsciously influence the way we think about ourselves and our behavior" (2016, p. 4).[8]

C. S. Lewis connected metaphor to the imagination and clarified that "imagination is the organ of meaning. Imagination, producing new metaphors or revivifying old, is not the cause of truth, but its condition" (2013, pp. 251–265). In other words, the imagination—the power of synthesizing images through metaphorical language—does not produce truth but makes the apprehension of truth possible.

[8] Their entire book centers on the idea that metaphors—journeys and pilgrimages, gardens and wildernesses, and buildings and walls—can reshape the way Christians accomplish education by framing the imagination in certain biblical ways.

Metaphor is the language that suggests the connection, and imagination is the faculty that interprets the connection and integrates it with the other "puzzle pieces." Thus, metaphorical language allows humans to understand abstract *truth* by connecting that truth to something within the realm of human experience. This is the power of imaginative language.

Additionally, Ryken explained that stories are extended metaphors. He suggested that stories "require active interpretation.... The narrative world that a storyteller creates by his or her selectivity of details is a picture of the world as the writer understands it, and of what is right and wrong in that world.... [A] story conveys much of its meaning by getting a reader to feel positively or negatively toward characters and events" (1990, p. 136). A story transfers meaning in the reader's mind and affections from the story presented to the reader's actual world. It puts the reader into the action so that the reader can compare it to the world that he knows and make a judgement—because he cares how the story will turn out. The reader must use his imagination to interpret the story. Ryken explained that "at the level of content, the differentia of literature is its presentation of human experience, as distinct from the conveying of information, facts, or propositions. Literature is incarnational. It enacts rather than states. Instead of giving abstract propositions about virtue or vice, for example, literature presents stories of good or evil characters in action" (1990, p. 8). Elsewhere Ryken wrote, "storytellers are never content with abstract propositions. Their impulse is to show, not merely to tell about an event. Stories help readers relive an experience in the order in which the events happened and as vividly as possible" (1990, p. 133).[9]

Roy Peter Clark exhorted writers to "learn the difference between reports and stories." He held that "reports convey information. Stories create experience. Reports transfer knowledge. Stories transport the reader, crossing boundaries of time, space, and imagination. The report points us there. The story puts us there" (2006, p. 124). A story, as opposed to a report, invests the reader's affections in the outcome. Thus, a story is a meta-

[9]Interestingly, in arguing that the Bible is story, he contrasts its form with that of a modern history book. He says, "Nor is most of the Bible organized as one expects history to be organized. This is not to question that the events recorded in the Bible are historically accurate. But these historical events are presented in narrative form, not as the accumulation of information like that found in *modern* history books" (134, emphasis added).

phor because it makes a transfer—in this case, it transfers *the reader* from his immediate experience to the world about which he reads. Stories, then, are an extension of the way language works through metaphorical transfer.

What "living" metaphors do—that reporting cannot—is offer language to connect various facets of reality (physical to metaphysical, concrete to abstract) to bring the reader's mind and affections together. Metaphors take an abstract idea and make the reader understand it through identifying him and his experience with that idea—knowing and feeling together. The reader becomes increasingly invested in the idea; his heart is oriented in a certain way because he has connected himself and the things he knows with what he is reading.

Modernism Abandons Metaphor

D. A. Carson characterized the rise of modernity by a new confidence in man's reason, man's sensory perceptions, and the infallibility of science (1996, pp. 58–64). Particulars instead of universals, physics instead of metaphysics, facts instead of form—these made the modern man, in contrast to pre-modern man. Richard Weaver wrote, "since the time of Bacon the world has been running away from, rather than toward, first principles, so that, on the verbal level, we see 'fact' substituted for 'truth'" (1948, pp. 12–13). Modernity told man that he never need look outside of himself—his experiences and his logic—for knowledge. He need not imagine the past, the future, or the metaphysical.

This scientific approach to knowledge affected not only content—fact mistaken for truth—but also the way that truth was presented. In short, modernism abandoned metaphor, both societal and linguistic. Charles Taylor noted that pre-modern society was built on "organic metaphor." Pre-modern societal order was a "type," or metaphor, of the hierarchy of God and the cosmos and stood "in analogy and interaction with the normative order of the soul." Modern society is just the opposite, ordered around individual rights and particulars without the metaphor of "hierarchal complementarity" (Taylor, 2004, pp. 95–100). As a result, moderns no longer understand or appreciate the necessity for metaphor.

Philosopher Eva Feder Kittay begins her book on linguistic metaphor with an historical overview of its use and understanding. She noted that "Locke's denunciations of figurative language set the tone for the philosophical disregard for metaphor—a position in which rationalist and empiricist were united" (1987, p. 1). Within a modernist philosophy of language, especially logical positivism, linguistic statements should be verifiable through science and reflect "the logical syntax of science" (1987, p. 7). Kittay further observed that most thinkers, the Romantics excepted, treated metaphor as a mere "enhancement" or "embellishment" for the "decoration or comparison" in language (1987, pp. 1, 4). With this view, metaphor was "dispensable in favour of a plainer expression or an explicit statement of similarity" (1987, p. 4). Kittay noted that this view of metaphor as mere ornamentation of language "requires a conception of [the] mind as a passive receptacle of perceptions." Instead, she argued that metaphor, "shaped through the imagination, ... is the linguistic means by which we bring together and fuse into a unity diverse thoughts and thereby re-form our perceptions of the world" (1987, p. 6). Ryken similarly observed that "the common assumption that scientific or expository discourse is precise while metaphor is vague is most inaccurate. Metaphor is as precise as a mathematical equation" (1982, p. 21).

C. S. Lewis (2013) likewise argued that modern man claims to be able to "think without metaphor"—to define and identify in literal language, independent of the need for metaphorical language. Lewis pointed out, however, that man cannot actually apprehend abstract concepts literally. One merely has the "power of changing the metaphors."

George Orwell argued that images make meaning clearer—and clarifying meaning through images is something at which modern writers abjectly fail. He gave an example of what the modern writer ("especially scientific, political, and sociological writers") would do to a verse from Ecclesiastes. He quoted Ecclesiastes 9:11 and then offered an alternate rendering of the verse in modern scientific language:

> I returned and saw under the sun, that the race is not to the swift, nor the battle to the strong, neither yet bread to the wise, nor yet riches to men of understanding, nor yet favour to men

> of skill; but time and chance happeneth to them all (King James Version, Ecclesiasts 9:11).

Here it is in modern English:

> Objective considerations of contemporary phenomena compels the conclusion that success or failure in competitive activities exhibits no tendency to be commensurate with innate capacity, but that a considerable element of the unpredictable must invariably be taken into account.

Orwell then lamented that "the whole tendency of modern prose is away from concreteness"—in other words, away from clarifying metaphor and toward meaningless and pretentious scientific and political jargon that strips humanity from the language (Orwell, 1984).

Arthur Holmes similarly stated that the modernist "scientific model" of language stands in contrast to the pre-modern philosophy of language of the humanities. He wrote, "the humanities do not just describe life and objectify it, they involve a man in it, they interpret it, and in interpreting it they express ideas and values that make up a world-and-life view and make a man what he is" (1971, p. 11). The scientific model, on the other hand, uses language to "communicate factual information. The locus of truth accordingly is the factual assertion" (Homes, 1971, p. 17). Restated, the modernist reduces language to mere objective facts. The "humanist"[10] interprets language in order to express value, worldview, and identity. Holmes asserted that the Christian humanist accomplishes this interpretive work through symbol, which "opens up the truth it 'shows' and helps men to see, to be truly human" (1971, pp. 11–17, 24).

Likewise, Richard Weaver argued that "the process of learning involves interpretation" and not just "facts" (1948, p. 12). Weaver asserted that only *modern* man believes that a bunch of facts can make him knowledgeable, when, in reality, the ability to interpret the facts is what gives man knowledge. Instead, Weaver suggested that "the staggering number of facts to which [the average man] today has access serves only to draw

---

[10] "Humanist" here refers to one concerned with the humanities or a liberal arts education, not secular humanism.

him away from consideration of first principles, so that his orientation becomes peripheral" (1948, p. 14).[11] Weaver's evaluation shows that by the mid-twentieth century, epistemology had completely shifted in favor of facts and scientific language. Weaver argued that "a developed culture is a way of looking at the world through an aggregation of *symbols* [emphasis added], so that empirical facts take on *significance* [emphasis added] and man feels that he is acting in a drama, in which the cruxes of decision sustain interest and maintain the tone of his being" (1948, p. 19). The more language moved from symbol to fact, the more man's orientation became "peripheral."

Evaluating Evangelical Textbooks

Based on the above understanding of linguistic imagery and the development of the imagination to orient the heart—and thus form worldview—educators need a way to be able to evaluate the degree to which Christian textbooks use imaginative language in order to successfully consider whether Christian textbooks do indeed present a biblical worldview through the eyes of the heart. Do Christian textbooks today effectively equip the next generation with a biblical worldview? Toward that end, this section offers three levels of imaginative language for use in evaluating textbooks.

Dead language. At this level, the language of the text does not attempt to engage the imagination. Instead, the text reports information by way of summary and accumulation of details and seeks to keep both the narrator and the reader neutral, often through the frequent use of passive voice (Clark, 2006, p. 124). In other words, reporting intentionally keeps a wall of separation between the reader and the events being reported. It tells what happened, remaining unconcerned about what happens. Reporting cares about particulars, not universals. It engages the mind without engaging the affections.

Weak language. At this level, the language of the text resorts to either cliché or faulty comparison, such as anachronism. Weak language

[11] Weaver wrote in 1948 and died in 1963, never having even dreamed of the internet.

alienates the reader by talking down to him through over-simplified or over-used language, causing the reader to disengage his imagination in disgust or annoyance (Wiersbe, 1995, p. 25). Alternately, weak metaphor makes a faulty transfer, recalling a concrete experience which actually causes the reader to *mis*understand the abstract concept.

Living language. At this level, the text uses metaphorical comparisons and story to engage both the mind and the affections to transfer the reader into an experience and make a connection with an abstract (and often universal) concept.

If evangelical educators are truly concerned with offering a biblical worldview in their textbooks, they must learn to rightly recognize and embrace imaginative, living language as the primary tool for worldview formation. They must judge their own worldview presentation not on the basis of their presuppositions but on the basis of their word pictures—their images, metaphors, and stories. These are the puzzle pieces that come together to form an imaginary, a worldview through which the next generation will live and move and have their being.

References

Abeka (n.d.). Why choose Abeka. Retrieved from https://www.abeka.com/homeschool/WhyAbeka/.

BJU Press (n.d.). About BJU Press. Retrieved from https://www.bjupress.com/about/.

Bryant, D. J. (1989). *Faith and the play of imagination: On the role of imagination in religion.* Macon, GA: Mercer University Press.

Carson, D. A. (1996). *The gagging of God: Christianity confronts pluralism.* Grand Rapids, MI: Zondervan.

Christian Liberty Press (n.d.). *Christian Liberty Press.* Retrieved from https://www.shopchris-tianliberty.com/christian-liberty-press/.

Clark, R. P. (2006). *Writing tools: 50 essential strategies for every writer.* New York, NY: Little, Brown and Company.

Crouch, A. (2008). *Culture making: Recovering our creative calling.* Downers Grove, IL: Inter-Varsity.

Frye, N. (1964). *The educated imagination*. Bloomington, IN: Indiana University Press.

Frye, N. (1985). "The expanding world of metaphor." *Journal of the American Academy of Religion* 53, (4) December, 585–598.

Gaebelein, F. E. (2009). *The pattern of God's truth: The integration of faith and learning.* Winona Lake, IN: BMH Books.

Gangel, K. (1995). In P. A. Kienel, O. Gibbs, & S. Berry (Ed.), *Philosophy of Christian school education.* Colorado Springs, CO: Association of Christian Schools International.

Green, G. (1998). *Imagining God: Theology and the religious imagination.* Grand Rapids, MI: Wm. B. Eerdmans.

Holmes, A. F. (1971). *Language, symbol, and truth. In Imagination and the Spirit: Essays in literature and the Christian faith*. Presented to Clyde S. Kilby. C. A. Huttar (Ed.). Grand Rapids, MI: William B. Eerdmans.

Holmes, A. (Ed.) (1985). *The making of the Christian mind: A Christian world view and the academic enterprise.* Downers Grove, IL: InterVarsity.

Kittay, E. F. (1987). *Metaphor: Its cognitive force and linguistic structure.* New York, NY: Clarendon.

Lakoff, G. & Johnson, M. (2003). *Metaphors we live by.* Chicago, IL: University of Chicago Press.

Leeds, M. (2005). *Imagination as a handmaiden to theology: An Evangelical appraisal of the role of imagination in theological methodology.* Ph.D. dissertation, Wake Forest, NC: Southeastern Baptist Theological Seminary.

Lewis, C. S. (2013). "Bluspels and flalansferes: A semantic nightmare." In *Selected Literary Essays*. New York, NY: Cambridge University Press, 251–265.

Master Books (2021). *Master Books: Overview*. Master Books Catalog. Retrieved from https://cdn.masterbooks.com/media/static_downloads/catalogs/2021-education-catalog.pdf.

Memoria Press (n.d.). *Memoria Press.* Retrieved from https://www.memoriapress.com/.

Moreland, J. P. & Craig, W. L. (2003). *Philosophical foundations for a Christian worldview.* Downers Grove, IL: IVP Academic.

Naugle, D. K. (2002). *Worldview: The history of a concept.* Grand Rapids, MI: Eerdmans.

Orwell, G. (1984). *Politics and the English language.* In George Orwell, *Why I Write.* New York, NY: Penguin.

Overman, C. (2006). *Assumptions that affect our lives.* Bellevue, WA: Ablaze.

Phillips, R. (2014). *The art and craft of Shakespeare: An interview with Peter Leithart.* Touchstone.

Ricoeur, P. (1981). *The rule of metaphor: Multidisciplinary studies of the creation of meaning in language* (R. Czerny, Trans.). Toronto: University of Toronto Press.

Ryken, L. (1990). "And it came to pass: The Bible as God's storybook." *Bibliotheca Sacra* 147, (586), 131–142.

Ryken, L. (1990). "I have used similitudes: The poetry of the Bible." *Bibliotheca Sacra* 147, (587), 259–269.

Ryken, L. (1982). "Metaphor in the Psalms." *Christianity and Literature,* 31 (3), 9–29.

Ryken, L. (1989). *The liberated imagination: Thinking Christianly about the arts.* Eugene, OR: Wipf & Stock.

Ryken, L. (1990). "With many such parables: The imagination as a means of grace." *Bibliotheca Sacra* 147, (587) 387–398.

Ryken, Leland. (1990). *Words of delight: The Bible as literature.* Bibliotheca Sacra 147, (585), 3–15.

Searle, A. (2009). *The eyes of your heart: Literary and theological trajectories of imagining biblically.* Eugene, OR: Wipf and Stock, 2009).

Simply Charlotte Mason (n.d.). *SCM curriculum.* Retrieved from https://simplycharlottemason.com/planning/curriculum-guide/.

Sire, J. W. (2014). *Naming the elephant: Worldview as a concept.* Downers Grove, IL: InterVarsity.

Sire, J. W. (1976). *The universe next door: A basic worldview catalog.* Downers Grove, IL: InterVarsity.

Smith, D. I. & Felch, S. M. (2016). *Teaching and Christian imagination.* Grand Rapids, MI: Eerdmans.

Smith, J. K.A. (2009). *Desiring the Kingdom: Worship, worldview, and cultural formation.* Grand Rapids, MI: Baker Academic.

Smith, J. K. A. (2013). *Imagining the Kingdom: How worship works.* Grand Rapids, MI: Baker Academic.

Smith, J. K. A. (2017). *Awaiting the King: Reforming public theology.* Grand Rapids, MI: Baker Academic.

Smith, J. K. A. (2011). *Worldview, sphere sovereignty, and desiring the Kingdom: A guide for (perplexed) reformed folk.* Pro Rege 39 (4), 15–24.

Taylor, C. (2004). *Modern social imaginaries*. Durham, NC: Duke University Press.

Taylor, C. (2002). "Modern Social Imaginaries." *Public Culture* 14 (1), 91–124.

Troxel, C. A. (2020). *With all your heart: Orienting your mind, desires, and will toward Christ.* Wheaton, IL: Crossway.

Wilson, D. (1991). *Recovering the lost tools of learning: An approach to distinctively Christian education.* Wheaton, IL: Crossway.

Vanhoozer, K. J. (2005). "Lost in interpretation? Truth, Scripture, and hermeneutics." *Journal of the Evangelical Theological Society* 48 (1), 89–114.

Vanhoozer, K. J. (2011). "Love's wisdom: The authority of Scripture's form and content for faith's understanding and theological judgment." *Journal of Reformed Theology* 5, 247–275.

Vanhoozer, K. J. (2016). *Pictures at a theological exhibition: Scenes of the Church's worship, witness and wisdom.* Downers Grove, IL: IVP Academic.

Vanhoozer, K. J. (2005). *The drama of doctrine: A canonical linguistic approach to Christian doctrine.* Louisville, KY: Westminster John Knox Press.

Veith, G. E. & Ristuccia, M. P. (2014). *Imagination redeemed: Glorifying God with a neglected part of your mind.* Wheaton, IL: Crossway, 2014.

Veritas Press (n.d.). *What makes us unique?* Retrieved from https://veritaspress.com/at-a-glance/what-makes-us-unique.

Weaver, R. M. (1948). *Ideas have consequences.* Chicago, IL: University of Chicago Press.

Wiersbe, W. W. (1995). *Developing a Christian imagination: An interpretive anthology*. Wheaton, IL: Victor.

Author Biography

Rebecca Aniol, Ph.D., is a pastor's wife and mother of four, whom she homeschools. She earned her doctorate in Educational Ministries from Southwestern Baptist Theological Seminary. She writes and speaks on education, discipleship, and the Christian imagination and leads expository women's Bible studies in her local church.

Building a Biblical Worldview for Children Through Spiritual Disciplines

June Lee, Ph.D.

Abstract: A biblical worldview cannot be taught overnight; it takes a lifetime. A biblical worldview is also comprehensive and cannot be limited to a particular aspect of life. Therefore, it is important to teach a biblical worldview at an early age, and it is significant for children to have the opportunities to learn through the interactions and experiences in their daily lives. The Bible calls parents and the church to teach children biblical truth and discipline to cultivate a life of faith. When parents and the church acknowledge the importance and urgency of teaching and leading children to God in their daily lives, they will be more likely to commit themselves to fulfilling their God-given calling. This article focuses on how parents and the church can teach a biblical worldview to the next generation and set fort the building blocks of a solid biblical foundation for children through bible reading, worship, prayer, service, and celebrating special occasions.

Introduction

When parents teach spiritual disciplines to their children, they take advantage of one of the greatest opportunities to cultivate a biblical worldview in the hearts of the next generation. This sort of family discipleship finds parents leading their children to love God and to grow in their relationship with the Lord through prayer, the Word of God, worship, and serving others. Parents devoted to obeying biblical passages such as Deuteronomy 6 and Ephesians 6, will diligently teach God's Word to their children while modeling a life of faithfulness and obedience through their own spiritual disciplines. It is critical that children witness the faith of their parents and see how God has worked in their lives (K. Jones, 2011).

Jewish communities provide meaningful examples of how religious groups transmit their values and practices to the next generation. Enduring a long history of persecution, their traditions and cultures have been passed down from generation to generation through challenging conditions (Dorff, 2012, p. 55). This legacy includes valuing children as precious to God and "the bearers of the tradition from one generation to another that strongly ties the past to the future" (Dorff, 2012, p. 23).

Jewish education consisted of religious education to teach Scripture (laws), walk according to the Scripture, know their forefathers' faith and deeds, and not transgress them while growing with the laws. Educating children in the ways of the Lord was one of the most important tasks of adults in the Jewish community. They believed education could not begin too early, should be engraved, and remain printed on children's minds. However, they never considered educating their children in the ways of the Lord an easy task. Intentional education required diligent work (Dorff, 2012, p. 28).

God's Design for the Family

God designed the family to be the primary learning community. He commanded parents to teach their children about Him (Strother, 2011; Baucham, 2007; May, et al., 2005; Stonehouse, 1998; Duncan & Johnson, 2004; Tripp, 1997; Rienow, 2009). Christian parents are to impress the hearts of their children with a love for God not only for living life on earth, but also in preparation for eternal life in Heaven (MacArthur, 2000; Farley, 2009; Rienow, 2009; Rienow, 2013).

As David Platt commented on Deuteronomy 6:4–9, he observed that faithful Jewish parents were to recite the Shema every day with their children (2013). As Peter Craigie wrote, "Shema was one of the most important prayers that the Jewish parents had to teach and recite with their children as the living affirmation of the faith" on everyday basis (1976, p. 168). The Shema was a constant reminder to the Israelites of their calling by God to receive "the divine relation in His words" (Wright, 1996, p. 95).

Harris described the Shema as the voice of God that is "distinctive, clear, and whole that orients people toward His way of life" (2016, p. 331).

The Deuteronomy 6 passage calls God's people to love Him with all their heart, soul and might (Deuteronomy 6:5). The commandment to love God with one's whole being requires complete obedience that generates concrete action (Wright, 1996). God commanded parents to internalize the Law in their hearts, which can be described as "the innermost being where genuine change and transformation can take place" (Turansky & Miller, 2006, pp. 12–13).

God commanded parents to live out what they teach to their children because children often model their thinking and behavior after their parents (Wright, 1996; Christensen, 2001; Hall, 1981; Harris, 2016; Loth, 2009; Kennemur, 2018). Parents are to encourage their children to love God by teaching them diligently about Him in both formal and informal settings. Formal teaching is structured or planned training in the Word. Informal teaching consists of capturing teachable moments to talk about God in the flow of ordinary everyday life. Both forms of teaching require intentionality with consistent parental teaching.

Intentionally Passing Down the Faith

Research found that parents who successfully passed on the faith to their children are usually involved in the following activities:

- Reading the Bible several times a week
- Taking part in a service project or church mission trip as a family
- Sharing their faith with unbelievers
- Encouraging teenagers to serve in church
- Asking forgiveness when they messed up as parents
- Encouraging their children's unique talents and interests
- Taking annual family vacations
- Attending churches with teaching that emphasizes the Word of God
- Teaching their children to tithe (LifeWay Research, 2021).

There are other common factors among parents who are more likely to influence their children's lives in biblical ways: highly religious, more involved in the lives of children in general, maintain positive parent-child and marital relationships, value education, and have greater commitment in modeling their own faith (Day, 2010; Smith & Denton, 2005). Ultimately, only God can transform one's life through the Holy Spirit. However, children's religious beliefs and devotion tend to be identifiable in specific types of families, relationships, traditions, and participation (Chandler, 2015; Smith & Denton, 2005).

Smith and Denton found that 8 to 10 percent of devoted young adults remain in their faith (2005, p. 110). Their common traits are described as follows:

> They are converted and pursuing spiritual growth through conversation, study, reading the Bible, prayer, small groups, and retreats. They possess a vital faith that recognizes God's presence and a spirit that reflects loving and hopeful attitude toward others and life. They are equipped and not entertained. They recognize God's call and actively practice their faith privately and publicly through integrating their faith to action, making moral decision, and participating in worship, ministries, and leadership. They live a life of service that care for others and reach out to others' need. Their parents preached the gospel to them (Bird, 2012, pp. 296–297).

Building a Biblical Worldview Through Spiritual Disciplines

A worldview can be defined as "a person's interpretation of reality and a basic view of life" (Naugle, 2002, p. 260). A worldview can be cultivated, and a biblical worldview can be built through spiritual disciplines. Beals defined *religious conversion* as a "changed worldview" and *religious education* as "the preparation for conversion and the bringing to conscious awareness all that is entailed in living the Christian life" (Beals, 2003, p. 122). Fostering faith through spiritual disciplines is crucial for building a biblical worldview.

Ephesians 6:4 instructs fathers to bring up their children in the ways of the Lord, which includes spiritual disciplines practiced and words spoken by fathers at home (Rienow 2009, p. 30). Although the father has the primary responsibility for disciplining children, the word "father" could be interpreted as both *father* and *mother*, who were to train and discipline their children in the ways of Lord (Lincoln, 1990). The word "bring up," ἐκτρέφετε (*ektrephete*), means nourish, feed, cherish, and bring up (Bock, 1996). The same word was used in Ephesians 5:29 to describe how Christ loved the church. Christian parents are to nurture their children in godly love in the same way Christ loves the church (Sear, 2008). The word "discipline," παιδείᾳ (*paideia*), refers to "the provision of guidance for responsible living" (Sear, 2008). Sear stated that it represents education and cultivation that involve "passing on culture, belief, conduct, and a comprehensive education" that "brings about enculturation of the covenant way of life" as instructed in Deuteronomy 6 (Sear, 2008, p. 62).

As Christian parents obey these Scriptures, they will nurture their children, bring them up in the discipline and instruction of the Lord, and teach the Word of God diligently to their children. Such faithful discipleship will include spiritual disciplines in the home that can lead to a biblical worldview. There are several spiritual disciplines for children and their families that can be practiced in order to foster a biblical worldview.

Bible Reading

The Bible is the central text for knowing about God, truth, and life for all Christians (Bunge, 2008, p. 355). To know God, one must know the story of the God who was, and is, and is to be active in a believer's life and history (Stonehouse, 1998, p. 208). Children need to keep on hearing and experiencing the whole unified and unfolding story of God repeatedly throughout their childhood (Allen, 2008, pp. 369–370).

God commanded Moses to instruct Israelites to celebrate ritual feasts every year (Stonehouse, 1998, p. 28). Israel was to tell the story of God faithfully to their children over and over again. This repeated rehearsal of God's faithfulness was a benefit for both children and adults because all were reminded about God's actions on their behalf throughout history. As they grew older, children would be able to go further in their understanding and reflection on who God is (Stonehouse, 1998, p. 208).

Reading the Bible together not only forms relational connectedness but also forges a spiritual attachment between the parents and children as they share "the experiences of the characters in the story, journeying with them, and learning from them" (Callahan, 2007, p. 255). God makes Himself known through His Word, and His people are invited to experience Him and to deepen their intimate relationship with Him (Smallbones, 2015, p. 83). Teaching children the Word of God is the key to knowing God (Trent, et al., 2003, p. 30). Paul commended Timothy's mother and grandmother for teaching Timothy the Word of God from childhood (2 Timothy 1:5, 3:14–16) for Scripture is able "to make you wise for salvation through faith in Christ Jesus" (2 Timothy 3:15, ESV).

(Family) Worship

Cultivating the spiritual discipline of worship in the life of a child helps to build a biblical worldview for the next generation while recognizing the truth that children are able to connect with God and experience Him. The central thrust of worship is "trusting God to be the leading force in a child's spiritual development" (Jonker, 2015, p. 299). Worship is an exciting way for children to know and learn about God because it allows them to enter the presence of God (Jonker, 2015, p. 305). It is absolutely crucial to focus on the Word of God during worship and to lead children to respond to God and His Word through prayer, praise, discussion, and obedience.

Most of all, an ongoing commitment, a faithful rhythm of worship is important. Christian parents must demonstrate their commitment to gather with the church family consistently for worship while also leading in regular family worship at home. Their attitude toward worship speaks volumes to their children (Bunge, 2008, p. 355). Children whose parents bring them to church and lead them in worship from an early age are more likely to grasp the reality of the presence of God, watch their parents publicly humble themselves before God, and experience the grace of the fellowship of God's people week after week throughout their childhood. Its cumulative effect on children's spiritual growth is beyond calculation (Stonehouse & May, 2010; Duncan & Johnson, 2004). These experiences will make a difference in times of trials and joy (Stonehouse & May, 2010, p. 175). Parents are also encouraged to put aside secular affairs and engage in regular family worship with their children at home (Duncan & Johnson, 2004, p. 13).

Prayer

Prayer is another important spiritual discipline that can help cultivate a biblical worldview for children. Prayer is a way to connect with God and recognize His presence (Jonker, 2015, p. 311). Prayer can open the door for children to experience God, maturing a child's relationship with Him (Stonehouse & May, 2010, p. 45). Children can learn through prayer that God is personal, omniscient, and omnipresent. They can talk to God as they speak to their parents or friends. They can speak to Him about anything, anytime, and anywhere.

Prayer habits and discipline established during children's early years can last a lifetime. Parents and adults can model an exemplary prayer life that flows from personal devotion as prayer habits are more caught than taught (Setran, 2014, p. 355). Experiencing God through worship and prayer within a family and faith community is important for building a biblical worldview and Christian identity (Stonehouse & May, 2010, p. 71).

Special Occasions

God prescribed religious rituals for the Israelites to observe each year. These rituals were a way to both commemorate what God had done for them and teach the faith to the next generation (Stonehouse, 1998, p. 28). God commanded the observance of three annual feasts in Deuteronomy 16: the Passover (16:1–8), the Festival of Weeks (16:9–12), and the Festival of Booths (16:13–17). The Passover celebrated God's deliverance of the Israelites from their slavery in Egypt. The Festival of Weeks celebrated the completion of the harvest. The Festival of Booths celebrated God's provision of booths to dwell in when the Israelites came out of Egypt to worship Him (Stonehouse, 1998, p. 29). These seven days of family and faith community events created several teachable moments for children. All the activities like songs and praise, Scripture reciting, storytelling, unusual taste of unleavened bread with bitter herbs, and spending nights in booths were experienced with family and faith community all together.

In American cultures, special occasions like Easter and Christmas are great opportunities for the spiritual training of children. Teaching the true meaning of these events—the resurrection of Christ and the incarnation of Christ—remains especially important in today's culture as commercial traditions like "Santa Claus and the Easter Bunny have all taken the place of Jesus" in Christmas and Easter (Trent et al., 2003, pp. 203–204). Indeed Christians have more reasons to celebrate these seasons because the Gospel message of Jesus coming to Earth as a Savior to die on the cross for our sins and rising again from the dead is the most wonderful gift of all. Children can still enjoy the excitement and anticipation involved in these seasons without having to follow the secularized culture's interpretation of these events (Romans 12:2). The traditions and values associated with special days like Easter and Christmas can be handed down from generation to generation and become part of a family's legacy of faith (Trent et al., 2003), further cultivating a biblical worldview for the next generation.

Mission and Service Projects

Children learn about Christian faith and values when they pay attention to those who are in need and find ways to help them in conjunction with their parents and faith community (Bunge, 2008, p. 355). Merton Strommen and Richard Hardel reported that children's "involvement in service projects proved to be a better predictor of faith maturity than participation in Sunday school, Bible study, or worship services" (2000, p. 95). A heart for missions, loving others, and learning how to meet people's needs should be a vital part of every Christian's lifestyle and a significant component in children's spiritual training (Dunagan, 2007, p. 16).

Missions and service projects also provide an opportunity to talk with children about financial responsibility: tithing from allowance, gathering offerings for churches and missionaries, helping those in need, and spending money wisely. These topics are important because "financial responsibility goes along with service to and love of others" (Bunge, 2008, p. 356). From an early age, many children are engaged in a consumer culture today. Studies shows that there are more shopping malls than schools in the United States and that the number one reason students drop out of college is credit card debt (Bunge, 2008, p. 356). It is crucial for Christian parents to help and teach their children from an early age to realize that everything they have belongs to God and they are to use their resources for His glory, the bottom-line purpose for their talents, time, and money (Dunagan, 2007, p. 154).

Conclusion

Winning the souls of the next generation by helping them build a biblical worldview through learning and experiencing the truth from an early age is critical. Parents need to model and teach spiritual disciplines to their children in order to foster this biblical worldview, praying that their children will follow Jesus Christ "as they join Christ in fulfilling their mission purpose on earth" (Ross, 2013, p. 26, 31). The teamwork of parents and the local church not only helps children build their life foundation and cultivate a biblical worldview, but also leads them to participate in God's plan for salvation (Ross, 2013; Haynes & Haynes, 2016).

References

Allen, H. C. (Ed.). (2008). *Nurturing children's spirituality: Christian perspectives and best practices.* Eugene, OR: Cascade Books.

Baucham, V. Jr. (2007). *Family driven faith.* Wheaton, IL: Crossway.

Beals, J. D. (2003). "The knowledge which comes by faith; A look at Evangelical conversion and worldview." *Reflections* 7, no. 1.

Bird, S. (2012). "Christian college students and emerging adulthood: Exploring or lost?" *Christian Education Journal* 13.

Bock, D. L. (1996). Luke. *Baker Exegetical Commentary on The New Testament.* Grand Rapids, MI: Baker.

Bunge, M. J. (2008). "Biblical and theological perspectives on children, parents, and 'best Practices' for faith formation: Resources for child, youth, and family ministry today." *Dialog: A Journal of Theology*, Volume 27, Issue 4, 348–360.

Callahan, L. V. (2007). "Turning down the noise: Reading and the development of spirituality in children." *Christian Education Journal*, 4(2), 252–267. https://doi.org/10.1177/073989130700400205.

Chandler, D. J. (2015). "Whole-person formation: An integrative approach to Christian education." *Christian Education Journal* 12.

Christensen, D. L. (2001). "Deuteronomy 1:1–21:9." *Word Biblical Commentary*, vol. 6a. Nashville, TN: Nelson.

Craigie, P. C. (1976). *The book of Deuteronomy, The New International Commentary on The Old Testament.* Grand Rapids, MI: William B. Eerdmans Publishing Company.

Day, R. D. (2010). *Introduction to Family Processes: Fifth Edition.* New York: Routledge.

Dorff, E. N. (2012). "The concept of the child embedded in Jewish law." In M. J. Bunge (Ed.), *Children, adults, and shared responsibilities: Jewish, Christian, and Muslim perspective*. New York, NY: Cambridge University Press.

Dunagan, A. (2007). *The mission-minded child: Raising a new generation to fulfil God's purpose*. Downer Grove, IL: IVP Books.

Duncan, L. & Johnson, J. (2004). "A call to family worship." *Journal for Biblical Manhood and Womanhood* 9, (1).

Farley, W. P. (2009). *Gospel powered parenting: How the Gospel shapes and transforms parenting*. Phillipsburg, NJ: P&R.

Hall, L. (1981). "Implementing Christian education in the home." *Christian Education Journal* 1.

Harris, S. L. (2016). "Between text and sermon; Deuteronomy 6:4–9, interpretation." *A Journal of Bible and Theology*, vol. 70(3).

Haynes, B. & Haynes, A. (2016). *Relentless parenting: The crucial pursuit of your teen's heart.* Nashville, TN: Randall House.

Jones, K. (2011). "The family in foundational years." In M. Anthony & M. Anthony (Eds.), *A theology for family ministries* (pp. 21–41). Nashville, TN: B&H Academic.

Jones, T. P. (Ed.). (2009). *Foundation for family ministry*. Nashville, TN: B&H.

Jonker, L. (2015). "Experiencing God: The history and philosophy of 'children and worship.'" *Christian Education Journal*, 12(2), 298–313. https://doi.org/10.1177/073989131501200204

Kennemur, K. (2018). "Nurturing faith in the home: Equipping parents of children to be spiritual leaders." In C. Shirley, *Family Ministry and the Church*. Nashville, TN: Randall House.

LifeWay Research (2021). "Young Bible readers more likely to be faithful adults." Retrieved from https://lifewayresearch.com/2017/10/17/young-bible-readers-more-likely-to-be-faithful-adults-study-finds/.

Lincoln, A. T. (1990). "Ephesians." *Word Biblical Commentary*, vol. 42. Dallas, TX: Word.

Loth, P. J. (2009). "Making your children into disciples of Christ." In P. J. Loth (Ed.), *Passing the torch of God's truth from generation to generation*. Glen Ellyn, IL: GCSSA.

MacArthur, J. (2000). *What the Bible says about parenting: God's plan for rearing your child*. Nashville, TN: Word.

May, S., Posterski, B., Stonehouse, C., & Cannell L. (2005). *Children matter*. Grand Rapids, MI: William B. Eerdmans.

Naugle, D. K. (2002). *Worldview: The history of a concept*. Grand Rapids, MI: William B. Eerdmans Publishing.

Platt, D. (2013). *Christ-centered exposition exalting Jesus in Matthew*. Nashville, TN: B&H Publishing Group.

Rienow, R. (2013). *Limited Church: Unlimited kingdom*. Nashville, TN: Randall House.

Rienow, R. (2009). "The role of the family in God's plan for the world. Retrieved from https://visionaryfam.com/the-role-of-the-family-in-gods-plan-for-the-world/.

Rienow, R. (2009). *Visionary parenting*. Nashville, TN: Randall House.

Ross, R. (2013). *Accelerate: Parenting teenagers toward adulthood*. Bloomington, IN: Cross Books.

Setran, D. (2014). "Igniting the family sacrifice: Cotton Mather and familial Christian education in Puritan New England." *Christian Education Journal* 11.

Smallbones, J. L. (2015). "Storymakers: A holistic approach to Bible reading and study." *Christian Education Journal*, vol. 12.

Smith, C. & Denton, M. L. (2005). *Soul Searching: The Religious and Spiritual Lives of American Teenagers*. Oxford: Oxford University Press.

Strother, J. (2011). "Making the transition to family-equipping ministry." In T. P. Jones (Ed.), *Trained in the fear of God*. Grand Rapids, MI: Kregel.

Stonehouse, C. (1998). *Joining children on the spiritual journey: Nurturing a life of faith*. Grand Rapids, MI: Baker.

Stonehouse, C. & May, S. (2010). *Listening to children on the spiritual journey: Guidance for those who teach and nurture*. Grand Rapids, MI: Baker Academic.

Strommen, M. P. (2000). *Passing on the faith: A radical new model for youth and family ministry*. Winona: Saint Mary's Press.

Trent, J., Osborne, R., & Bruner, K. (2003). *Parents' guide to the spiritual growth of children: Helping your child develop a personal faith*. Carol Stream, IL: Tyndale House Publishers.

Tripp, P. D. (1997). *Age of opportunity*. Phillipsburg, NJ: P&R Publishing.

Turansky, S. & Miller, J. (2006). *Parenting is heart work*. Colorado Springs, CO: David C Cook.

Wright, C. (1996). *Deuteronomy, New International Biblical Commentary*. Peabody, MA: Hendrickson.

Author Biography

June Lee, Ph.D., received a master's degree in Childhood Education and a Ph.D. in Childhood Education with a Minor in Family Ministry from Southwestern Baptist Theological Seminary (SWBTS). She has served as a teaching fellow at SWBTS and is currently serving as the director of First Steps Preschool at Katy's First Baptist Church in Katy, Texas.

Considering the Challenges of Teaching the Problem of Evil to Teenagers and a Critique of Available Resources

Eddy Wu

Abstract: The Problem of Evil is considered one of the strongest arguments against the Christian faith and teenagers cannot ignore this reality of evil and suffering. This article will argue that the Problem of Evil has not been made comprehensively accessible for teenagers as the current available literature is too intellectually simplistic. A brief survey of three popular resources available for students on the topic reveals a lack of intellectual depth. Thus, considering more philosophically rich positions will expand and deepen the Problem of Evil apologetic conversation for teenagers.

Introduction

In Christian apologetics, the Problem of Evil (PoE) is considered to be one of the strongest arguments against the Christian faith. The reality of evil is difficult to ignore as our news networks and social media platforms bombard us with stories of immense suffering and evil committed by man and nature alike. Teenagers[1] are not shielded from this unfortunate reality

[1] Throughout this article, "teenagers" will often refer to young men and women whose age range from youth ministry and even to college. While terms like "young adults" may also be applicable, using the term "teenager" will help to include a larger demographic as "young adult" will seem to entail certain social and life responsibility that is not quite yet expected of these individuals. Teenage years begin in middle school, continue through high school, and include some of the college or early young adult years.

as they receive sobering updates from their phones and other avenues at a blistering rate. As such, teenagers are not exempt from wrestling with the difficult reality of evil in their own immediate lives, the lives of others around them, and the wider global community.

However, teenagers reside within a unique intellectual maturity period of their lives. While they are not considered fully developed adults (mentally and physically), teenagers also should not be treated as young children who are unable to intellectually grasp theological truths or have honest struggles with difficult topics. Within this strange period of adolescence, many teenagers are eager to engage in apologetical conversations, including the PoE, but in a manner that recognizes the student's intellectual capabilities. To this end, are there PoE resources available for teenagers to meet this expectation? In this article, I will argue that the Problem of Evil has not been made comprehensively accessible for teenagers as the current available literature focused on teenagers is too simplistic in its treatment of the problem.

First, I will quickly present the basics of the PoE discussion. Next, I will briefly survey three of the more popular apologetic resources available for teenagers[2] and critique these resources on their viability for teenagers. Finally, I will suggest a new approach to the PoE for teenagers that considers the teenager's intellectual capabilities as more capable than the current literature may suggest.

More Than One Problem of Evil

Before the PoE literature can be examined, the PoE argument must be identified. Generally, the PoE is divided into two conversations: the

[2] The descriptor I am using to qualify the selected texts is "available for teenagers." The texts are not books for working with teenagers such as Sean McDowell and J. Warner Wallace's *So the Next Generation Will Know: Preparing Young Christians for a Challenging World* or Hillary Ferrer's *Mama Bear Apologetics: Empowering Your Kids to Challenge Cultural Lies*. Those books are helpful resources for adults who want to work with teenagers on apologetics. Rather, the selected texts are books that may not be specifically written for teenagers but are accessible enough for a teenager to read.

emotional problem and the intellectual problem.[3] The emotional problem deals with the existential questions and personal despair that arise from experiences with evil. The emotional aspect will not be the focus of this article. Instead, the intellectual discussion, which looks for an explanation for why God allows evil and so much of it, will be my primary focus. This narrow focus on the intellectual side of the topic does not diminish the importance of addressing the emotional side. Rather, establishing an intellectual foundation of the PoE can help assist with the emotional side as Bruce Little explained, "Those who would suggest that theodicy is a poor use of one's time and energy should understand that without a theodicy, comforting those who suffer has no enduring foundation. Effective Christian ministering to those who are suffering requires proper understanding of the relationship of suffering to God" (Little, 2010, p. 12). The availability of this "proper understanding" for teenagers is precisely what is in question.

The intellectual argument can be further divided into two distinct types of arguments: the logical and the evidential. Most versions of the logical argument from evil usually follow a format similar to this:

1. If God is all-powerful (omnipotent), He could destroy evil.
2. If God is all-loving (omnibenevolent), He would destroy evil.
3. Evil exists.
4. Therefore, God does not exit.[4]

While there are different ways to formulate the logical argument, the strategy remains the same across the variations. The logical argument implies that there is a contradiction between the existence of God as traditionally understood (affirming God's attributes of omnipotence, omniscience, and omnibenevolence) and evil. Although the logical argument

[3] A more extensive explanation of this distinction between the emotional and intellectual (as I have chosen to label them) can be found in John S. Feinberg, *The Many Faces of Evil: Theological Systems and the Problems of Evil* (Wheaton, IL: Crossway Books, 2004), 21–27. Feinberg, instead, named the emotional as the "religious" and the intellectual as the "theological/philosophical."

[4] This is my preferred method for stating the logical argument from evil due to its simplicity with three premises and a conclusion and represents a format that is most often encountered in public. Other versions of the same logical argument can be found in Michael L. Peterson, *God and Evil: An Introduction to the Issues* (Boulder, CO: Westview Press, 1998) on page 23 and in Douglas Groothuis, *Christian Apologetics: A Comprehensive Case for Biblical Faith* (Downers Grove, IL: InterVarsity Press, 2011) on page 629. Certainly, the two books by Peterson and Groothuis are not the only sources that cover the logical argument but they both present the standard structure of the logical argument.

is still present today, philosophers widely agree that Alvin Plantinga's free will defense (Plantinga, 1974) "adequately rebuts the logical problem of evil" (Peterson, 1998, p. 41). Thus, the logical argument already has a viable response accepted by both atheist and Christian alike.

On the other hand, the evidential argument for evil is considered the more difficult and pressing argument for the Christian to intellectually address. Made popular by William Rowe (who calls himself a "friendly atheist"), the evidential argument from evil differs from the logical argument in its argument type. While the logical argument is a deductive argument, the evidential argument is an inductive argument based on probability where the amount and intensity of evil in the world makes God's existence improbable. Rowe provides two examples of evil, E1 and E2,[5] to demonstrate that there are evils that could be considered gratuitous (there are no goods that result from the evil which can justify God permitting the evils to occur) which would count against God's existence. Thus, the evidential argument must be examined on its own merit.

Why is it so important to distinguish between the two versions of the PoE when considering how to discuss this topic with teenagers? While this differentiation may seem specifically reserved as an academic task, introducing teenagers to the PoE requires this distinction be made to help clarify the argument. The logical and evidential arguments are approached and answered differently because the arguments themselves are structured differently. Thus, while teenagers should not be expected to engage with the technical nuances of the discussion, introducing and clarifying the distinction between the logical and evidential versions helps teenagers recognize

[5] Rowe's examples of evil, E1 and E2, are brought up to highlight instances of evil and suffering in both the natural world and as a result of human suffering that does not seem to result in a corresponding good to justify God allowing them to occur. E1, also referred to as "Bambi," is a hypothetical scenario where the reader is asked to imagine lightning striking a tree in some distant forest which causes a forest fire. In the midst of this forest, a fawn is trapped, horribly burned, and ultimately dies after several days of agony. E2, also referred to as "Sue," comes from a true story from the *Detroit Free Press* of January 3, 1986. The details of the account are difficult to read and process so I will only provide a brief summary. The report details a young five-year-old girl who was beaten, raped, and then ultimately strangled to death by her mother's boyfriend. The first case, E1 with the fawn in the forest, demonstrates a fictional but yet believable case of natural evil. The second case, E2 with the young girl, demonstrate a real case of moral evil. By using both examples, Rowe wants to argue that God could (and should) have prevented these evils from happening since there is no observable corresponding good that results from these events.

which responses/theodicies are satisfactory. Additionally, teenagers should find confidence in Alvin Plantinga's response to the logical problem as a sufficient and widely accepted defeater.

Survey and Critique of Available Literature for Teenagers

With the problem defined and the two versions of the argument established, we can now turn our attention to reviewing the available literature for teenagers. There are a few things to be aware of before diving into the resources. First, the literature selected can only be considered a fraction of the available Christian apologetic literature. The works I have chosen to examine represent apologetic resources that I believe are considered more popular and also accessible to teenagers in their content and their style. Additionally, one will notice the PoE is only one chapter from these texts. Second, more weight will be given to how each of the resources address the intellectual side of the PoE conversation rather than the emotional/existential. While the emotional/existential aspects of the PoE are certainly important, this article's focus remains on whether the existing literature on the topic is available and helpful for teenagers to intellectually process the argument itself. Finally, although I will not focus on this aspect, one should be mindful that the PoE can influence other theological beliefs. When a person studies the PoE, they find that this conversation may cause them to reconsider their thoughts about who God is, humanity's relationship with God, and one's understanding of the biblical text. Therefore, one's response to the PoE must be theologically acceptable to orthodox Christian doctrines.

Furthermore, as I begin to survey the apologetic texts on the PoE, each will be critiqued in the following areas. The goal is to ensure that the apologetic work is comprehensive enough on the subject and, yet, also accessible for the teenager. First, does the apologetic work distinguish between the two problems: the emotional/religious vs the intellectual? This distinction also continues to whether the logical and evidential are properly identified and differentiated. Then, what responses/theodicies does the author offer for the PoE? Finally, is the author's presentation of the PoE accessible and comprehensive for teenagers and, if not, where does the author's presentation fall short?

Tim Keller's *The Reason for God* and *Walking With God Through Pain and Suffering*

Tim Keller and his two apologetic books, *The Reason for God* (2008) and *Walking with God through Pain and Suffering* (2013), are the first to be examined. In both books, Keller engages with the PoE where the topic is given a short chapter in the former work as part of a larger general apologetic resource and significant attention in the latter as the primary focus of the entire work. *The Reason for God* is often considered a more popular book as it was a *New York Times* bestseller and is more often recommended as an entry-level apologetic resource. However, Keller's latter work, *Walking with God through Pain and Suffering*, is just as important since it provides more foundational details on his view.

Writing primarily from a pastoral perspective, Keller's focus in both books is not on providing detailed intellectual answers for the PoE. Rather, Keller encouraged the suffering Christian to "live life well and even joyfully against the background of these terrible realities" (2013, p. 3). However, Keller did distinguish between the emotional and intellectual problems as he stated, "Some find unjust suffering to be a philosophical problem, calling into question the very existence of God. For others it is an intensely personal issue" (2008, p. 22). Additionally, Keller also explicitly identified the two versions of the PoE when as he wrote, "There are two forms that the argument against God from evil can take. They have been called the logical argument and the evidential argument" (2013, p. 88). Thus, Keller did identify the distinction between the different types of arguments.

Although Keller's books primarily have a pastoral tone, he still provided some introduction to the various responses/theodicies offered by theists. In *The Reason for God*, Keller argued that the PoE "is perhaps an even greater problem for nonbelievers" (2008, p. 26) and appealed to Jesus' suffering on the cross as the reason for seeing that our sufferings are not in vain. In his more recent work, *Walking with God through Pain and Suffering*, Keller provided several of the standard philosophical responses such as: John Hick's soul-making theodicy, Augustine and Plantinga's free will theodicy/defense, and Stephen Wykstra's skeptical theism (Keller, 2013, pp. 89–99). While Keller did present these three responses, ultimately, he claimed that theodicies "always fall short ... of explaining all suffering" (2013, p. 95).

How does Keller's work on the PoE fare as a resource for teenagers specifically? Keller's work on the PoE must always be viewed from within the context that he is writing. Keller wrote these books as a pastor addressing those who are struggling with evil and suffering in their lives and see these calamities as reason to leave the Christian faith. As such, Keller wrote to address the emotional/religious side of the discussion rather than engage in the philosophical discussion.

Keller did well to highlight the distinctions in the various types of arguments (emotional vs. intellectual and logical vs. evidential) and he even managed to introduce some of the more common responses (free will theodicy, soul-making, and skeptical theism). It is clear that Keller is aware of the larger academic conversation and of the more nuanced debate around some of the theodicies/defenses provided. However, Keller's quick dismissal of theodicies as an acceptable response limited the intellectual scope of his presentation as he confined himself specifically to defenses. As a result, much of Keller's work on the PoE is restricted to showing that the argument of evil does not disprove the Christian faith and that the atheist worldview still has to address the reality of evil regardless. Seemingly, Keller's preferred response is to appeal to Christ's suffering and some form of a skeptical theism defense.

While Keller certainly should be applauded for his pastoral approach in addressing the emotional side of the PoE, ultimately his intellectual work would leave a teenage reader wanting. Keller's position relied heavily on a defense that highlighted failures of the atheist position to provide a satisfactory answer, or an attitude of trusting God to bring some greater good out of the evil. Unfortunately, this leaves teenagers in a precarious position where their spiritual walk may be stabilized but the intellectual struggle with evil and suffering still remains. Just because the atheistic position on the PoE is weak, the Christian does not automatically claim victory as the problem continues to persist for the believer. Thus, Keller's position, while helpful from an emotional/religious aspect, fails to provide the intellectual depth that teenagers need to process the PoE beyond showing the deficiencies with the opposition.

Rebecca McLaughlin's *Confronting Christianity*

The second author is Rebecca McLaughlin and one of her more recent books on apologetics, *Confronting Christianity: 12 Questions for the World's Largest Religion* (2019). McLaughlin's book, and her other apologetic work *10 Questions Every Teen Should Ask (and Answer) about Christianity*, serve as general apologetic texts that (similar to Keller) touches on a number of different apologetic topics as she forms her defense of the Christian faith. McLaughlin represents a more popular level apologetic work accessible for teenagers. Similar to Keller, McLaughlin's work on the PoE is found in one chapter of the book.

McLaughlin recognized the difference between the emotional and intellectual discussion when she affirmed that "Philosophers through the ages have offered defense for the idea of a loving omnipotent God in the face of suffering" (2019, p. 197). Unfortunately, she did not distinguish between the logical and evidential arguments, though she did make a passing mention of Plantinga's free will defense (McLaughlin, 2019, p. 197).

Adopting a similar focus as Keller, McLaughlin aimed to demonstrate that other worldviews (such as the atheistic or Buddhist worldview) fail to provide a sufficient explanation for evil and suffering in the world. More than just the failures of the other worldviews, McLaughlin also highlighted how Jesus experienced suffering and thus "suffering and sickness are rolled up together with sin and guilt and loaded onto the Messiah's back" (2019, p. 201). McLaughlin referenced that a punishment response does not work with an appeal to Job since "the amount of suffering a person endures is not proportional to his or her sin" (2019, p. 203). Instead, she relied on elements of a soul-making theodicy combined with eschatological greater good responses (2019, pp. 205–206).[6]

Bearing many similarities to Keller, McLaughlin's approach reminds us that Jesus was not excluded from suffering but endured suffering so that we may share a "special intimacy with him" (McLaughlin, 2019, p. 201). McLaughlin's arguments do not emphasize an intellectual engagement on the topic nor do they present the various theodicies/defenses available.

[6] McLaughlin does not provide much explanation for the theodicy she presents. Thus, my naming of her response as the soul-making theodicy mixed with eschatological greater-good principles is based on my interpretation of her text.

McLaughlin did highlight the weaknesses of other worldviews, in part, to put forth the Christian faith as a superior worldview for addressing the reality of evil and suffering. But, just pointing out the insufficiency of another worldview (like atheism or Buddhism) to adequately explain evil and suffering does not necessarily prove the Christian worldview can intellectually hold its own ground against the charges of the PoE.

While McLaughlin may help the reader see that Christ does intimately relate to our sufferings, she did not explicate the arguments she hinted at in her chapter (such as the punishment theodicy, soul-making, and skeptical theism). Her treatment of the PoE largely ignores the intellectual discussion and would leave teenagers without the necessary tools to think through the intricacies of the problem. McLaughlin was correct when she stated, "Our pain is real and urgent. It refuses to be soothed by faraway hope. Neat, theological answers will not do. But neither are they all that Christianity offers" (2019, p. 199). But McLaughlin could supplement her emotional address with a more robust discussion of the intellectual conversation.

Douglas Groothuis's *Christian Apologetics*

Finally, my survey will end by examining Douglas Groothuis's (2011) substantial apologetic text, *Christian Apologetics: A Comprehensive Case for Biblical Faith*. As its name implies, Groothuis's text is indeed a comprehensive book on Christian apologetics that covers a variety of apologetic topics. Groothuis looked to expand apologetics beyond simplistic answers as he wrote, "simply saying 'Jesus' when someone asks why you have hope in times of suffering is to fail to give a full apologetic" (2011, p. 24). Additionally, he recognized that philosophy is crucial to apologetics as he stated, "A Christian-qua-apologist, then, must be a good philosopher (even if not a professional philosopher). This is nonnegotiable and indispensable" (2011, p. 27). Thus, although he only devoted one chapter to the PoE (like Keller and McLaughlin), one should expect Groothuis to engage with the philosophical (or what I have been calling the intellectual) discussion in detail.

Unlike Keller or McLaughlin, Groothuis's treatment of the PoE leans more toward the intellectual direction than the emotional. This is not to say that Groothuis ignored the emotional aspect of the PoE as he discussed Christ's suffering on the cross near the end of the chapter, but rather, his focus remained primarily on the intellectual side. He did provide a brief distinction between the logical and the evidential arguments. Not only did Groothuis distinguish between the two different versions of the argument, he also correctly identified that Plantinga has largely defeated the logical argument with his free will defense (Groothuis, 2011, pp. 629–631).

Groothuis took two approaches as he provided his response to the PoE. Like Keller and McLaughlin, Groothuis first locked at how five unsatisfactory worldviews (atheism, a finite god, God lacking in omnibenevolence, the nonexistence of evil found in Advaita Vedanta Hinduism and Zen Buddhism, and finally karma and resurrection) attempt to address the PoE. Ultimately, all five of the worldviews examined fail to provide a satisfactory response due to internal logical consistency or denigration of God's divine attributes.

After critiquing the five other worldviews, Groothuis offered three responses specifically "tackling the inductive or evidential problem of evil" (2011, p. 631). First, he presented a kind of free will theodicy predicated on compatibilist freedom rather than the traditional libertarian freedom espoused by Plantinga or Swinburne. Next, he presented a greater-good defense that combined elements of the soul-making theodicy with skeptical theism. Finally, Groothuis concluded by quickly looking at how Jesus' death on the cross and subsequent resurrection provides "[t]he single greatest example of good triumphing over evil ... " (2011, p. 644). Thus, for Groothuis, there are sufficient reasons for why God would allow evil and suffering in our world.

How does Groothuis's treatment of the problem fare? Overall, Groothuis engages with the PoE conversation with significant intellectual depth. From this chapter, teenagers would receive a good introduction to the topic and its various arguments (such as the distinction between the logical and the evidential or the free will defense). From an introductory perspective, Groothuis provides the most focus on the intellectual conversation out of the works surveyed.

However, even for all the positives, his work could be further developed. While his explication of a free will defense/theodicy introduces the reader to the different types of free will (compatibilism vs. libertarianism), he does not always help make the connection to how the explanation of free will resolves the problems posed by evil and suffering.

Additionally, while Groothuis's introduction of theodicies and defenses should be applauded, there is a certain nuance to the subject that is missing. Groothuis's focus on providing defenses rather than a theodicy never allows the Christian to consider the full theological implications since a defense is only concerned with what might be the case. This sole focus on defenses also limits any substantial engagement with the various responses (such as the theological and philosophical problems with a greater-good response). It would benefit teenagers more to understand the strengths and weaknesses associated with each position.

These three resources surveyed are critiqued to be incomplete as accessible and comprehensive resources for teenagers on the PoE. The authors often overemphasize the emotional side of the problem to the neglect of presenting a comprehensive view of the intellectual conversation. This is not to say that the emotional aspect of the PoE should be ignored, but rather, the apologetic works often exclusively focus on one side to the detriment of the other. When the authors do engage with the intellectual side, their treatment is normally focused on the logical problem or presenting some version of the free will defense or a form of the greater-good theodicy/defense. There are more Christian apologetic works available. The ones examined in this article represent a small portion of the available literature.[7]

Considering a New Way Forward

If the resources on the PoE presently available for teenagers are not complete, then what does such a resource look like? In this section, I will offer some brief thoughts on what must be considered when presenting the PoE to teenagers and how to structure that conversation in the future. These thoughts are certainly not conclusive and will require more

[7] It is important to highlight that this survey does not cover the resources I would consider to be too philosophical dense or technical. Those resources were not considered as a viable example since a strong background in philosophical terminology and logic or Bayes Theorem would be required to read them.

research[8] to determine how best to develop resources for teenagers. Overall, I will seek to present a step forward in the conversation that highlights some of the important parts of the problem for teenagers.

When we consider teaching to teenagers, we cannot ignore the cultural and educational contexts in which teenagers are situated. First, as it relates to culture, teenagers are acutely aware of the reality of evil and suffering. Their personal electronic devices and social media feed a torrent of news. Second, resources on the PoE directed for teenagers cannot assume that teenagers are intellectually ill-equipped to think through this topic. This presumption would set the engagement bar far too low for teenagers who have shown the capability to learn high-level concepts in their math, science, and English courses. If teenagers are already challenged academically in other subjects, they can also be theologically and philosophically challenged on the PoE. Since teenagers cannot elude the problem, they should be equipped to think and address it in a manner that acknowledges their current stage in life. While there are interesting philosophical discussions that arise from the PoE (such as Bayes Theorem or debating the different types of free will), teenagers need resources that comprehensively cover the important matters while remaining accessible.

Foundationally, teenagers should be able to distinguish between the emotional vs. intellectual problems and also the logical vs. evidential distinction. Recognizing the first distinction, between emotional and intellectual, helps the teenager understand which argument he is facing (addressing the emotional PoE focuses on counseling and the intellectual looks at the logic). Alvin Plantinga recognized the importance of this distinction as he wrote, "Faced with great personal suffering or misfortune, he may be tempted to rebel against God, to shake his fist in God's face, or even to give up belief in God altogether. But this is a problem of a different dimension. Such a problem calls, not for philosophical enlightenment, but for pastoral care" (Plantinga, 1974, pp. 63–64). Similarly, the distinction between the logical and evidential argument highlights the different method an op-

[8] By research, I am thinking of surveys or polls to better gauge how teenagers currently do understand the PoE. Such a survey would evaluate the important aspects in the PoE that teenagers should be expected to know, examine responses the teenager would provide, understand why the teenager thinks their answer is theologically/philosophically acceptable, and consider resources they have previously encountered.

ponent may use. Then, it would be helpful to acknowledge and explain the widely accepted defeat of the logical problem by Plantinga's free will defense.

Once the foundation has been established, teenagers need to know how Christians have responded. Teenagers should be introduced to various positions such as: Plantinga's free will defense, a free will theodicy such as Augustine, the traditional greater-good theodicy, Hick's (2010) soul-making theodicy, Wykstra's (2017) skeptical theism, and even a lesser-known theodicy like Little's (2004) Creation-Order theodicy. Chad Meister and James Dew's two edited books, *God and the Problem of Evil: Five Views* (2017) and *God and Evil: A Case for God in a World Filled with Pain* (2012), would be good resources to consider as Meister and Dew compile these various Christian responses. While some of these responses will need to be adapted for the teenage audience, these responses expose the teenager to a range of available options to consider for themselves.

Not only should the teenager be exposed to more, but responses should also be honestly critiqued on their respective strengths/weaknesses and theological implications. Without any honest reflection, teenagers may assume their response can be held without any significant opposition, but this is not the reality of the PoE conversation. All responses will have their respective strengths and weaknesses that may intersect with one's held theological beliefs. Critical reflection on a position challenges the teenager to think deeper about the response they have chosen to hold to and why.

As an example, let's briefly examine what could be considered the most common response by Christians to the PoE: the classic greater-good theodicy (Little, 2004, p. 24). As summarized by Bruce Little, the greater-good theodicy is "[t]he idea that the only evil allowed by God is the evil from which He can bring about a greater good or prevent a greater evil … " (2010, p. 58). The greater-good theodicy seems a natural response as God bringing good out of evil *prima facie* seems to match with His divine attributes of omnipotent and omnibenevolence. Additionally, the greater-good theodicy appears to have strong biblical support from passages such as: Genesis 50:20; Romans 8:28; and Job 42:12–13 where Job receives more than he lost. Thus, the greater-good theodicy is often an attractive response since it affirms God's sovereignty and has biblical support.

The greater-good theodicy should be considered a viable option for the Christian as it does have a strong historical foundation (Little, 2004, pp. 31–57). However, a blind acceptance of the theodicy as the only legitimate response ignores the associated philosophical and theological pitfalls. Little is a helpful critic here as he provides several substantial critiques of the greater-good theodicy (Little, 2010, pp. 60–78; Little, 2004, pp. 109–126). He highlights the theodicy's inability to numerically adjudicate the amount of good necessary to allow evil, our inability to connect a specific good with a specific evil, and he even provides a different interpretation for the biblical passages normally referenced as support for the theodicy. This critical analysis of the greater-good theodicy should also be taught to teenagers.

Teenagers are intellectually capable of engaging the PoE conversation beyond the bare basics. Yet, the majority of resources available for teenagers on the topic do not provide teenagers with in-depth philosophical and theological tools. This does not mean that teenagers should be given the thickest and most technical philosophy works on the PoE. Rather, a middle approach should be considered that comprehensively covers the topic while remaining accessible to teenagers.

Conclusion

The reality of evil and suffering continues to persist in this world. Teenagers will have to biblically address the question of how God could allow such horrendous evils and sufferings to occur for themselves and others. Teenagers should be equipped with the tools and resources needed to significantly engage this problem. The apologetic works by Keller, McLaughlin, and Groothuis were all examined as examples of resources that often emphasize the emotional side of the PoE without presenting a comprehensive view of the intellectual conversation. Work needs to be done to "translate" these apologetic works on the PoE to a format that is both comprehensive and accessible for teenagers. Perhaps, youth and family pastors can take up the baton in teaching the philosophical and theological concepts to teenagers in their context.

References

Baring, R. V. (2010). Analyzing empirical notions of suffering: Advancing youth dialogue and education. *Religious Education* 105:2, 157–174.

Clark, M. (2017). *The problem of God: Answering a skeptic's challenges to Christianity*. Grand Rapids, MI: Zondervan.

Eatmon, S. (2021). Why Teenagers Need a Theology of Suffering. Retrieved from https://rootedministry.com/blog/why-teenagers-need-a-theology-of-suffering.

Feinberg, S. J. (2004). *The many faces of evil: Theological systems and the problems of evil*. Wheaton, IL: Crossway Books.

Ferrer, H. M. (Ed.). (2019). *Mama bear apologetics: Empowering your kids to challenge cultural lies*. Eugene, OR: Harvest House Publishers.

Groothuis, D. (2011). *Christian apologetics: A comprehensive case for biblical faith*. Downers Grove, IL: InterVarsity Press.

Hick, J. (2010). *Evil and the God of love*. England: Palgrave Macmillan.

Keller, T. (2008). *The reason for God: Belief in an age of skepticism*. New York, NY: Penguin Group.

Keller, T. (2013). *Walking with God through pain and suffering*. New York, NY: Penguin Books.

Little, B. (2010). *God, why this evil?* Lanham, MA: Hamilton Books.

Little, B. (2004). *A creation-order theodicy: God and gratuitous evil*. Lanham, MA: University Press of America.

McDowell, S. & Wallace, J. W.(2019). *So the next generation will know: Preparing young Christians for a challenging world*. Colorado Springs, CO: David C Cook.

McLaughlin, R. (2019). *Confronting Christianity: 12 hard questions for the world's largest religion*. Wheaton, IL: Crossway.

Meister, C. & Dew, J. K., Jr. (Eds.). (2017). *God and the problem of evil: Five views*. Downers Grove, IL: InterVarsity Press.

Meister, C. & Dew, J. K., Jr. (Eds.). (2012). *God and evil: A case for God in a world filled with pain*. Downers Grove, IL: IVP Books.

Moreland, J. P. & Craig, W. L. (2017). *Philosophical foundations for a Christian worldview*. 2nd ed. Downers Grove, IL: InterVarsity Press.

Peterson, M. L. (1998). *God and evil: An introduction to the issues*. Boulder, CO: Westview Press.

Plantinga, A. (1974). *God, freedom, and evil*. Grand Rapids, MI: Wm. B. Eerdmans Publishing Company.

Wykstra, S. (2017). A Skeptical Theist View. In C. Meister & J. K. Dew Jr. (Eds.), *God and the Problem of Evil* (pp. 99–127).

Author Biography

Eddy Wu is a Ph.D. student in Apologetics and Culture at Southeastern Baptist Theological Seminary, while also working as an IT operations manager.

Practitioner Insights

The *Southwestern D6 Family Ministry Journal* editorial board helped design the uniqueness of this journal. This section entitled Practitioner Insights offers you a look at family ministry from practitioners engaged in preschool, children, student, college, adults, or senior ministry. The practitioner reflections do not submit to the same academic peer review process but still pass through multiple editors before becoming part of the volume. We believe this section will allow insightful ministry leaders the chance to present an areafacing the church today.

Bible Courses Back in Public Schools: Discipling and Training Students With the Gospel for Elective Credits

Gady Youmans, D.Ed.Min.

Problem: *How do we educate and train students that stay busy when pastors only have a couple hours each week at church, and many parents lack the knowledge to do so themselves?*

I have observed a struggle among churches regarding how to educate students in knowledge and application of biblical instruction in their lives. We live in a time when school and extracurriculars are top priorities, parents lack discipleship themselves (thus failing to disciple their kids), and churches struggle to cram everything in on Sundays and Wednesdays with no real way to hold students accountable for their progress in learning. As a student pastor, I found myself realizing that students do not have to go to church, nor can I make them read/study their Bibles. If parents were not involved in a student's growth in Christ, my efforts seemed to fall on complacent and "busy" ears. This is where God showed me that there is a way to address these concerns in a single concerted effort that can produce results far beyond what the typical church education ministry can accomplish in American student ministries.

What if there was a way to offer Bible courses as elective credit for our *public high school* students every single school day? What if we could make Bible study accountable to a grade on a school transcript? What if we could multiply the church's efforts to teach and equip past Sunday and Wednesday Bible study to every day of the week for over an hour in an academic setting? What if we could equip students with the equivalent to a "minor in biblical studies" before they graduate high school? What if we could give parents fodder to discuss with their kids over the dinner table such as, "What did you learn in Bible class at school today and how does that apply to our lives today?" What if I told you all of this was perfectly legal in the United States and it is happening right now? Would you want to see this in your church's community?

Solution: *There's a way to put biblical education back in schools: Released Time Education*

Released Time Education (RTE) is a SCOTUS tested opportunity that originally dates back more than 100 years allowing parents to remove their students from the public school each day for religious instruction.[1] The SCOTUS in 1952 ruled that as long as students were voluntarily taking the courses, the religious instruction was off campus, and such programs were funded 100% via private funds (no school funding), then such religious instruction was legally protected nation-wide. It is estimated that thousands of such programs exist in the United States and millions of students have participated over the years in RTE programs.

How to Take Advantage of RTE: *Start a Christian Learning Center in your community.*

I founded the Sweet Onion Christian Learning Center (CLC), a 501(c)(3) non-profit organization, in 2013. The problems I had previously recognized were plaguing my mind, but it made perfect since to start a ministry unlike anything else in the area apart from starting a private Christian school. While I recruited a board of directors from the community, local churches could easily form a CLC ministry via their local denominational association or community partnerships with other evangelical churches.

While I cannot speak to the specific requirements of each state school system and/or local boards of education, I can offer insight as to how multiple public-school systems in my area have responded to the CLC efforts

[1] Further state-by-state specifics regarding the legalities for RTE can be found at the School Ministries Inc. website. https://releasedtime.org/. States vary in the process by which non-accredited educational organization elective credits may or may not be accepted. Seeking guidance from one's own local board of education regarding this process and ensuring the local board that all legalities will be adhered to helps ease the fears of litigation by opposing groups. Practically speaking, the local school systems are simply accepting "private school" credits to be transferred onto the public-school transcript. Providing courses at the Christian Learning Center that already utilize public school accepted course codes goes a long way in mitigating any confusion for accepting of credit.

and how such an opportunity has benefited the students. Since our first class in 2014, we have partnered with three different public-school systems, enrolled hundreds of students (at no cost to students) and have never experienced a situation that has caused legal concern for either the CLC or any partnering school system.

The Georgia Department of Education established course codes for the following courses: History and Literature of the Old Testament (and New Testament), Comparative Religions, Personal Financial Literacy, and Psychology.[2] Each of these courses can be taught *on* the public-school campus *by* public school teachers but must be taught objectively with no evangelistic or religious stances made or implied. But through the CLC ministry, local boards of education in Georgia accept such RTE courses as long as the students meet daily like a regular class and the CLC teacher has either the professional expertise to justify the elective credit or has appropriate academic credentials.[3]

What are the discipleship advantages of having these courses taught in your community? Multiplying the impact of church and home discipleship, students are further challenged in their public-school education, which includes the accountability of a grade and the repetitive exposure of roughly 180 school days per year. Providing academic courses to public school students puts the Bible back into schools in a manner that students would expect to be challenged given the academic setting. From a discipleship perspective, the courses equate to a "minor in biblical studies" and can easily establish a foundation for a Christian worldview. Pastors, imagine a student ministry full of students who are being equipped in Bible knowledge, theology, stewardship, apologetics, and counseling/discipleship. Now, imagine the impact such a group can have in and through the local body of Christ at your churches.

[2] The above listed course names are the course names for the Georgia Department of Education. For my ministry, I use these course codes but name these courses differently on my syllabuses. History and Literature of OT/NT are referred to as *Old/New Testament Survey*. Comparative Religions is renamed *World Religions and Apologetics*. Personal Financial Literacy is renamed *Biblical Finances and Stewardship*. Psychology is renamed and taught as a *Biblical Counseling and Discipleship* course.

[3] Bible college graduates and pastors that hold seminary degrees would easily meet the minimum academic requirements for several of these classes. However, a school system may be leery to award credit for the personal financial literacy and psychology courses if the instructor does not have academic standing or significant experience in those fields.

A student that participates in our CLC would receive roughly 360 days or 540 hours of instructional time in the off-campus[4] classroom if they take four different CLC courses in high school. Translate that into Sunday School and Wednesday night Bible study time, and that would equate to seven years of perfect attendance at the local church (yet they get that in just two school years at the CLC). The Scriptures cannot be expounded upon with such consistency, exposure, grade accountability, and at an academic discussion level and not have an impact on those involved. The approach and methods we have employed to develop the CLC ministry I oversee have seen phenomenal results in heart change and transformation, all for which I give glory to God.

Results at the Sweet Onion Christian Learning Center

Programs do not change lives, only God transforms sinners into followers of Jesus. However, I have been intentional to evaluate our CLC model, while helping others begin CLC's in their communities, with the intention of everything being done for the glory of God and to further Kingdom work. Below are some of the highlights I have consistently seen in our CLC ministry:

- Unchurched students will take a Bible class at school, including atheists and those of other faiths in order to ask questions and get answers.
- Salvations are frequent in the classroom with 1 in every 6 students enrolled surrendering to Christ during class.
- CLC students' knowledge of the Word is exponentially greater than their peers, as attested to by local youth pastors and parents as they observe their CLC students' growth. Heart transformation is a day-to-day occurrence in class.

[4]The biggest legality to abide by is the off-campus aspect of the ministry. Our CLC meets at the closest feasible church to the high school and utilizes the church's student center(s) and/or other available classroom space. Also, transportation to/from the public school must be provided by the CLC via a van/bus or the students participating must be able to drive themselves/carpool with parental consent. For schools with 7 periods a day, transportation time may cut into instructional seat time, but for block scheduling the seat time is relatively a non-issue. Our CLC has operated in three different public-school systems under both schedules with no problems.

- Students claim that CLC courses are the most impactful and influential courses in their high school career that prepare them for Christian living and adult life.
- Families are assisted in discipling their students by having school work to discuss at home, students sharing how they are growing in class, and parents learning alongside their student via discussions at home.[5]
- The CLC has facilitated opportunities for parents to seek pastoral counsel and biblical insight from the Bible teacher(s). Some parents have been saved while others have sought to simply learn deeper things of the Lord vicariously through their student.[6]
- Churches are helped with educating their students and training in discipleship by partnering with the CLC so that students can receive a foundation of Bible knowledge in the classroom and church service efforts can be used to pour into students in a complimentary way that disciples families.

Summary

Students do not have to go to church, but they do have to go to school. Not every student can afford a private Christian education, but they have the legal right to get religious instruction during the school day. The question is whether or not the church in America will take full advantage of RTE and make the most of an amazing opportunity to disciple the next generation of believers in the knowledge and ways of the Lord.

[5] Parents are the primary disciple-makers of their kids, while the church and school play complimentary roles. CLC's can be a source of parent and student disciple-making and equipping when parents engage in the student's course content through helping them study, discussing applications to what they are learning in the classroom, and parents seeking to further their biblical education through their local church ministry. Parents at our CLC have often commented to me that helping their kids study for Bible assignments or just discussing the daily content over dinner also helps them to grow in their faith given that many parents have never taken a biblical course in an academic setting.

[6] One of the opportunities CLC has had to directly impact adults in the community is through offering Bible studies at local churches and/or mid-week opportunities to learn the same content students learn in the classroom. Adults consistently comment, "I wish I could take your classes. Do you offer any adult courses?" By replicating CLC type courses in the local church, the ministry is encouraging and modeling enhanced educational ministry opportunities in the local church for adults in areas of Bible knowledge and discipleship skills.

Author Biography

Gady Youmans, D.Ed.Min., is the founder and executive director of the Sweet Onion Christian Learning Center and the lead pastor of Word of Life Baptist church in Vidalia, Georgia. He holds a D.Ed.Min., M.A. in Christian Education, and M.A. in Biblical Counseling from Southwestern Baptist Theological Seminary.

Ways to Disciple Your Children "As You Go"

Rich Griffith, D.Min.

Discipleship should not be something scary or time consuming. In fact, when we consider Deuteronomy 6, much of discipleship is "as you go," or as you do life together. Deuteronomy 6:7–9 reads, "Impress [the commandments of God in His Word] on your children. Talk about [His Word] when you sit at home and when you walk along the road, when you lie down and when you get up. Tie [God's commandments] as symbols on your hands and bind them on your foreheads. Write them on the doorframes of your houses and on your gates" (NIV). Notice that each of these verses imply an "as you go" way of discipleship with your children. Further, these guiding statements are both for the home and the community as indicated by the doorframes and gates.

Discipleship and theology are simply speaking about the things of God and how his Word applies to our lives. Do not worry about your kids knowing more than you do or asking difficult questions. Discovering answers together are, in and of itself, discipleship.

It is also important to remember to do things that are simple, functional, and sustainable. Here are some practical ideas for discipling your children as you go:

At Home

- **Read through the Psalms**. My son and I drive together to his school and my work. We work our way through the book of Psalms, one Psalm each morning. He will read the Psalm out loud and then we discuss what is written and how we can apply it to our lives. The Psalms allow us to find our comfort in God, but they also allow us to see that it is okay to have a whole range of emotions we can express toward God. As we finish, either he or I pray. You can also mix it up by doing the same thing with Proverbs or the Gospel of John.
- **Develop a family mission statement**. My family's mission statement is to "love God, love each other, love others, and relieve

suffering whenever and wherever possible in the name of Jesus." We then try to go out several times a year and join in some sort of local community mission work in keeping with this statement.

- **Learn about spiritual disciplines and put them into practice**. Solitude, fasting, giving, prayer, being present, worship, and Bible study remain some of the most important spiritual disciplines in the Christian life and discipleship opportunities in the home. For instance, when children are older, teach them to fast from electronics or even food for a short period of time. Talk to them about the discipline of giving and use periods of the year (Christmas, birthdays, Thanksgiving, etc.) and encourage them to think about how the family can give to others. Families can also incorporate times of joint prayer, praise, and Bible study in the home through family worship.
- **Practice active listening**. As parents, we spend a lot of time teaching, correcting, and disciplining. It comes with the job. However, we need to set a time apart, at least one time a week, to just listen to our kids. This means no distractions. Put the phone away. Listen to listen, not answer. Look your child in their eyes. Lean forward. Really listen. Repeat back what they are saying. This lets your child know that you are listening. Ask simple questions like, "how do you see God at work in your life?"
- **Pray with intention**. Find a time each day where intentional prayer (not the rote mealtime prayers) can be expressed together. Just as Jesus taught His disciples how to pray, prayed in front of them, and prayed with them, parents can teach their children to pray, pray in front of them, and pray with them, inviting them to grow in their own prayer lives.
- **Do a family video prayer journal**. Sort of like TikTok, families can record their challenges (prayers) and hopes (praises). Keep these in a video file. Save them to the Cloud (or have individual flash drives for each month) and after six months or so, go back and review your videos and see how God has moved. Do this as a family so that, as your kids get older, they will remember, and have access to, the legacy of valuing prayer and praises in your family.

- **Have each family member choose a favorite Bible verse**. One way that parents can disciple their children "as they go" is to encourage their children to choose a favorite Bible verse. Families can then discuss and memorize these verses together and even find creative ways to post them throughout the home or on the "doorframes of your house."
- **Look for teachable moments**. Some of the best teachable moments occur naturally. Whether it is a question that comes up from watching a movie together, a song lyric that turns into an impromptu discussion, or a simple observation of people as you go, parents can use these moments to engage in conversation and ask their children, "What do you think about that?" "What do you think God would say about it?"
- **Enjoy a regular family game night or something else special**. Families can enjoy great conversations as they play a game or just go out for ice cream. Take time to be present with your children intentionally and have fun. Loving your family and spending time together is just another practical way to show them the love of Christ "as you go."

In Church and in Your Community

- **Attend worship together**. This sounds simple, but the modern Western church is far too often segregated by ages during worship services. However, even young children can learn to worship with their parents and older generations in the church. Prior to the service, challenge your child to listen for at least one thing they can learn. After the service, compare what you and your child learned and talk about it. Worshipping together with the church family is just one more way to disciple your children "as you go."
- **Form family connection groups**. Be intentional about creating and connecting with church family affinity groups. It is amazing the amount of support you get from each other. Be intentional about planning a quarterly get together. Maybe it is a picnic, a cookout, or a casual meeting at Dairy Queen. A game night also works really well. Invite "adopted" singles, grandparents, aunts, and uncles from the church family to join your family. These groups can gather

weekly, monthly, seasonally, or during the summer. Such gatherings allow both parents and children to build Christian community with other believers and other generations.

- **Serve in a ministry area together at your church**. Whether it is singing, running AV, greeting, taking up the offering, or serving in children's ministry, serving together as a family is how you train up the next generation of leaders as you teach them to serve alongside adults. Christian children and youth are the church now, not just of the future, and if we do not engage them now through owning ministry, they will not be around to be "the Church of the future."
- **Find a spiritual mentor for your child outside the home**. The earlier you do this the better because your child will come to a point in their lives where they will have situations they do not want to talk to you about, either because they are embarrassed or they do not want to disappoint you. An outside mentor becomes a partner in your family's discipleship ministry, providing a Titus 2 example of intergenerational discipleship.
- **Surround your child with other godly adults**. Other godly adults investing in the discipleship of your children may include your children's minister, youth leader, a coach, a teacher, "adoptive" grandparents, aunts, and uncles. The fact is that the more Christian, caring adults you have involved in different capacities, the more your child will be surrounded by Christian nurture. People often panic if you ask them to "mentor" a child because they think they are not equipped, so I use the term "spiritual encourager." My son has a spiritual grandma named Mrs. Harriett. Jamie will go over and help with yard work or other tasks and Mrs. Harriett takes time to play games, teach Jamie how to cook or bake, and most importantly, to listen to him. God intends for the entire community to nurture and spiritually guide our young people.

As you can see, discipleship does not have to be difficult. You do not need to be a Bible scholar to disciple your children. My sons and I have often learned deep spiritual concepts together. By listening to them process God's Word as we go, I learn a great deal from my kids, making me a better parent, pastor, and professor.

Having more natural spiritual conversations with my sons allows me to point them to Jesus Christ every day. In Him we are free to do the things that work for our family. We do not have to do them perfectly, because His righteousness covers our sins and shortcomings. Following the guidance of His Word and His Spirit, you too can establish rhythms that work for your family and allow you more and more opportunities to disciple your children "as you go."

Author Biography

Rich Griffith, D.Min., is associate professor of youth ministry at Toccoa Falls College. He has two master's degrees (Theology and Organizational Leadership) and a doctorate in "Youth, Family, and Culture" from Fuller Theological Seminary. He is an author, speaker, coach, and part-time pastor. He is a single dad of three adopted sons.

The Family: Cultural and Biblical Views

Travis Flanagan

Introduction

This paper will examine the concept of the family through two lenses, that of our current culture and that of the Bible. These two sections will then be followed by some concluding remarks providing implications and applications. The overarching goal is to derive, straight from the inspired Scriptures, God's intended purpose and design in creating the family and to understand how we then shall live.

A Cultural View of the Family

Needless to say, everyone's family is different. This means that within the discussion of a cultural view of the family, there are so many talking points. While space does not allow for a complete discussion of every issue, the major topics to be dealt with include marriage and divorce, and same-sex relationships/marriages.

Marriage and Divorce

In the next major section, we will see that marriage was instituted by God Himself. At this point, however, we must note how marriage has become regulated by the government. In the state of Texas, for instance, there are a number of requirements to be met before becoming legally married in the eyes of the state. First, you must pay a fee and obtain a marriage license, provide a form of proper identification, be at least 18 years of age and, wait at least seventy-two hours after obtaining the license to be married (TexasAttorneyGeneral.gov).

Along with the "how" to get married in our culture today, it will be helpful to note the reasons "why" individuals choose to become legally married. A 2019 survey by the Pew Research Center revealed the following motivations for marriage: love (90%); companionship (66%); wanted to make a formal commitment (63%); wanted to have children someday

(31%); it made sense financially (13%); it was convenient (10%); they or their partner were pregnant (6%) (Pew Research, 2019). While the motivations for marriage differ for each individual and couple, we should also note that some couples choose to never even get married.

A 2020 Gallup poll asked the following: "When a couple plans to spend the rest of their lives together, how important is it to you that they legally marry?" Thirty-eight percent responded, "very important," twenty-six percent responded, "somewhat important," while thirty-six percent responded, "not too important" or "not important at all" (Jones, 2020). If less of the population values marriage, it only makes sense that many who are already married may choose divorce. Divorce, like marriage, contains a legal aspect. Nevertheless, it is now easier than ever to file for a divorce. In Texas, all of the paperwork can be filed online. State law now allows for divorce papers to be served by e-mail or even social media. The United States now has the sixth highest divorce rate in the world. Fagan and Churchill wrote, "Only a few generations ago, American culture rejected divorce as scandalous. Today, law, behavior, and culture embrace and even celebrate it" (2012, para. 2).

Statistics show that half of the children in the United States will witness the end of a parent's marriage (Fagan & Churchill, 2012). Divorce not only impacts adults, but children as well. Ninety percent of divorced mothers have custody of their children and 43% of children in the United States are being raised without their fathers.

Today's culture appears to value marriage less and less. This is seen both in the number of divorces as well as the decreased desire for marriage in the first place. While a divorce is between two adults, a divorce truly impacts the entire family.

Same-Sex Relationships and Marriages

Falling under the umbrella of our culture's understanding of the family is the somewhat new practice of same-sex marriage. The Supreme Court's ruling in the case of Obergefell vs. Hodges on June 26, 2015 legalized the practice in the United States. Upon the fifth anniversary of this ruling (in the year 2020), USA Today reported that about 300,000 same-sex couples had been wed in those five years. Many other individuals in same-sex relationships are not married. A 2019 American Community

Survey conducted by the US Census Bureau showed a total of 980,000 same-sex couple households. Data released by Gallup on June 1, 2022 revealed that American support for same-sex marriage had risen steadily for twenty-five years and stood at an all-time high of 71% in 2022 (McCarthy, 2022). These numbers demonstrate our culture's strong shift away from a biblical view of marriage and the family.

A Biblical View of the Family

When one opens the pages of Scripture it should be clear that, from the beginning, God had a purposeful plan for the family. God created both male and female in His very image (Genesis 1:27). After creating male and female in His image, God immediately blessed them and issued what is referred to by theologians as the creation mandate: "Be fruitful, multiply, fill the earth, and subdue it. Rule the fish of the sea, the birds of the sky, and every creature that crawls on the earth" (Genesis 1:28, HCSB). We see here that God had a very purposeful *design* (male and female) as well as a very purposeful *plan* (to be fruitful, to multiply, to fill the earth and subdue it).

Turning to Genesis 2, we get a closer look at God's creation of man (Genesis 2:7) and woman (Genesis 2:21–22). Once God created man and woman, the text says that God brought the woman to the man and the man replied, "This one, at last, is bone of my bone, and flesh of my flesh; this one will be called 'woman,' for she was taken from man" (Genesis 2:23, HCSB). This is what some consider to be the very first marriage ceremony. Woman was given by God to the man, and the verse which follows explains, "This is why a man leaves his father and mother and bonds with his wife, and they become one flesh." (Genesis 2:24, HCSB).

When we read Genesis 1–2, we should have no doubt that the marriage relationship is God's intended plan for males and females to carry out the creation mandate. In many situations, however, both inside and outside of the church, the cultural reality is far from the biblical standard. In what follows, we will see that God's design for marriage and the family includes one man and one woman for life; children born to and raised by a married mother and father; and families who worship together at church and in their homes.

God's Design for Marriage

First and foremost, God's design for marriage includes an exclusive covenant between one man and one woman until death do they part. We have already seen from Genesis 1–2 that the marriage relationship was designed by God for a man and a woman, not for two men or for two women. This idea of a man and a woman being married for life was re-emphasized by Jesus in Matthew 19 when some Pharisees tested Him by asking Him what the Law says about divorce. Jesus responded by reminding them of God's design for marriage:

> "Haven't you read," He replied, "that He who created them in the beginning made them male and female," and He also said: "For this reason a man will leave his father and mother and be joined to his wife, and the two will become one flesh? So they are no longer two, but one flesh. Therefore, what God has joined together, man must not separate" (Matthew 19:4–6, HCSB).

Jesus goes back to the very beginning. Before the Law, and even before the fall of man, there was marriage, ordained by God Himself (Blomberg, 1992, p. 290). This, according to Jesus, implies that every marriage should be seen as being ordained by God and should therefore be permanent (Köstenberger & Jones, 2010, p. 77).

When marriage is not viewed as being directly from the Lord, it loses much of its designed sacredness. When marriage is seen as a regulation of the government rather than an institution of God, there is less hesitation to separate it.

God's Design for Children and Parents

It should be clear from the creation mandate that God's plan and purpose for marriage and family includes children. Psalm 127:3–5 reminds us that "Sons are indeed a heritage from the LORD, children, a reward. Like arrows in the hand of a warrior are the sons born in one's youth. Happy is the man who has filled his quiver with them" (HCSB). While there are cases which prevent couples from having children, the biblical pattern and general expectation is for married couples to bear and raise children. And if God's design is for marriages to last, and it is also God's design for married couples to have children, then God's plan certainly involves children whose fathers and mothers are both actively involved in their upbringing. Scripture addresses the unique roles of fathers and mothers.

In the household codes of Ephesians and Colossians, Paul specifically addresses fathers and exhorts them to bring up their children "in the training and instruction of the Lord" (Ephesians 6:4b, HCSB). A clear warning is also issued to fathers: "don't stir up anger in your children" (Ephesians 6:4a, HCSB), and "do not exasperate your children, so they won't become discouraged" (Colossians 3:21, HCSB). Köstenberger wrote, "While children ought to obey both parents ... fathers bear special responsibility for disciplining their children" (2010, p. 107).

Paul also has much to say regarding the role of women and mothers in the Pastoral Epistles. In Titus 2, he instructs the older women of the church to set a proper example and to teach the younger women "to love their husbands and children, to be sensible, pure, good homemakers, and submissive to their husbands, so that God's message will not be slandered" (Titus 2:4b-5, HCSB). Paul also highlights Timothy's mother's role in his discipleship, passing down her faith (2 Timothy 1:5) and teaching him the Scriptures from childhood (2 Timothy 3:14–15).

Men and women, husbands and wives, fathers and mothers each have a unique role to fulfill, one that was designed by the perfect plan of God. This plan finds both the father and the mother present in the lives of their children. Köstenberger summarized this well when he wrote, "God's ideal is a godly father and a godly mother complementing one another in raising children in proper discipline and love" (2010, p. 273).

God's Design for Family Worship and Discipleship

A biblical family not only lives together, but also worships together. While the local church is the place for the weekly gathering of the saints, families should also be enjoying worship and discipleship together in their homes. We find this in Deuteronomy 6:4–9. This passage makes it clear that parents are to be the main disciplers and worship leaders of their children.

Deuteronomy 6 calls parents to disciple their children in the morning and in the evening, at home and while traveling. Families should, therefore, set aside time each day for family worship. Donald Whitney suggested families spend time together praying, singing, and reading the Word (Whitney, 2016). Whitney stated that "without some regularity, structure, and purpose, bringing our children up 'in the discipline and instruction of the Lord' is one of those things that we can assume we are doing but never actually do as well as we might think. Consistent, father-led family worship is one of the best, steadiest, and most easily measurable ways to bring up children in the Lord's 'discipline and instruction'" (2016, p. 25).

How Then Shall We Live?

We have examined a cultural view of marriage and family coupled with a biblical response. We live in a fallen world filled with broken marriages and broken families. Nevertheless, God's Word gives us clear guidance when it comes to these issues. Therefore, in what follows, a series of addresses will help us answer the question: In light of God's design for marriage and family, how then shall we live?

- **To the unmarried:** Approach dating and marriage carefully and biblically. Seriously consider the commitment God expects in a marriage relationship.
- **To the happily married:** Do not take what you have for granted. Thank God daily for the spouse He has given you (Proverbs 12:4; 18:22).
- **To the unhappily married:** Fight and pray for your marriage. Very seldom is divorce the best answer. Statistics show that those who are unhappily married and divorce are still unhappy or even less happy years later, while those who stayed in their marriages had on average moved past the bad times and reached a happier stage (Baslwick & Baslwick, 2007, p. 299).

- **To those interested or engaged in a same-sex relationship:** Understand this is neither God's ideal nor His design and understand this is sin. A same-sex relationship is not the proper way to enjoy a God-ordained and God-honoring marriage and family.
- **To parents:** Live your life in a way that models the Gospel to your children. Redeem every moment and use them as discipleship opportunities. Be intentional about worshipping together with your family at church *and* at home.
- **To children:** As an act of obedience to God, seek to honor and obey your parents in all things.
- **To the church:** Be prepared to stand in the gap. Marriages and families are falling apart all around us. Let us be a church that biblically guides the unmarried, prays for the unhappily married, and celebrates the happily married. Let us equip parents to be the best disciplers of their children. And let us fill the void for the many children and students who do not have fathers and/or mothers present in their lives.

References

Baslwick, J. O. & Balswick, J. K. (2007). *The family: A Christian perspective on the contemporary home*, Third Edition. Grand Rapids, MI: Baker Academic.

Blomberg, C. L. (1992). *Matthew*. NAC vol. 22. Nashville, TN: B&H Publishing, 1992.

Fagan, P. F. & Churchill, A. (2012). The effects of divorce on children. *Marriage and Religion Research Institute*. Retrieved from https://marri.us/wp-content/uploads/The-Effects-of-Divorce-on-Children.pdf.

Jones, J. M. (2020). Is marriage becoming irrelevant? *Gallup*. Retrieved from https://news.gallup.com/poll/316223/fewer-say-important-parents-married.aspx.

Köstenberger, A. J. (2003). Marriage and family in the New Testament. In K. M. Campbell (Ed.), *Marriage and Family in the Biblical World*. Downers Grove, IL: IVP Academic.

Köstenberger, A. J. & Jones, D. W. (2010). *God, marriage, and family: Rebuilding the biblical foundation*, 2nd ed. Wheaton, IL: Crossway.

McCarthy, J. (2022). Same-sex marriage support inches up to new high of 71%. *Gallup*. Retrieved from https://news.gallup.com/poll/393197/same-sex-marriage-support-inches-new-high.aspx.

Pew Research (2019). Retrieved from https://www.pewresearch.org/social-trends/2019/11/06/why-people-get-married-or-move-in-with-a-partner.

Texas Attorney General (n.d.). Retrieved from https://www2.texasattorneygeneral.gov/files/cs/8marriage.pdf.

Whitney, D. S. (2016). *Family worship*. Wheaton, IL: Crossway.

Author Biography

Travis Flanagan is a blessed husband and a thankful father of three. He serves as the pastor of students and families at Plymouth Park Baptist Church in Irving, Texas.

Book Reviews

The book reviews submitted offer a critique of some of the latest family ministry titles. If you would like to see a title reviewed in the future, please submit at least two copies of either the book or galley copy. (Publisher's PDF proof is acceptable if not yet published or to galley stage).

Navigating Student Ministry: Charting Your Course for the Journey. Edited by Timothy McKnight. Nashville, TN: B&H Academic. 2022. 349 pp. $34.99. paper.

Review by Frank Trimble, director of training and consulting at Family Time Training in Littleton, Colorado.

Tim McKnight, Ph.D., serves as associate professor of Christian Studies at Anderson University and pastor of Mosaic Church of Anderson in South Carolina. His experience in academia, pastoral ministry, and military service make him a fitting editor for this in-depth guide for student ministers. *Navigating Student Ministry* is intended to function as a practical guide that student ministers can use as they begin or continue their vocational journey (p. 3–4).

McKnight begins the book with a biblical defense of student ministry in chapter one. In chapter two, Sam Totman describes the vocational call of the student pastor and the qualifications necessary for the role. In chapter three, McKnight discusses the importance, quality, and substance of the student minister's daily life. Chapter four features Chandler Vannoy's explicating the essential elements of leadership development in student ministry. In chapter five, McKnight treats the importance and function of the student ministry team. Paul Kelly, in chapter six, engages adolescent development and its implications for student ministry practice. In a similar tone, Karen Jones, in chapter seven, addresses the unique cultural and social realities of teenagers. In chapter eight, Timothy Paul Jones discusses the value and role of the family in connection to student ministry. Justin Buchanan, in chapter nine, articulates the significance of evangelism in the lives of students and the student minister. In chapter ten, R. Scott Pace presents the importance and holistic nature of discipleship in student ministry. Totman, in chapter eleven, evaluates the use of technology in student ministry and offers a strategy for how to do so well. In chapter twelve, Troy Temple engages in what he calls "Student Ministry Next," examining the adjustments and innovations of student ministry's past to best approach its future. In the concluding chapter, McKnight outlines a plan of implementation based on the contents of the book. Two appendices regarding historical precedents for age-organized ministry and the importance of active partnerships with parachurch organizations close the volume.

Navigating Student Ministry supplies a thorough treatment of various topics related to student ministry practice. The contributors have offered their respective expertise for the benefit of student ministers. One of the more laudable traits of the book is its insistence upon the cruciality of families and the larger congregation regarding the spiritual development of teenagers. Additionally, the volume highlights just how essential it is that the student ministry be connected to the congregation—even in vision and mission.

Although the book features plenty of helpful content, some of its claims may give readers pause. For example, in chapter one, readers may find themselves asking what student ministry is. That is, what does the author mean by the term? In addition, though McKnight clearly holds a high view of Scripture (chapter ten), the passages he treats do not directly support the institution of student ministry. Noteworthy is the author's use of Deuteronomy 6:4–9 as a foundational passage supporting student ministry. McKnight derives much application from the fact that the entire nation of Israel was gathered to hear Moses. This national gathering is used to support Levitical and community involvement in the discipleship of children (p. 14). However, more exegetical work concerning Deuteronomy 6 is needed to substantiate the author's claims.

Once McKnight moves to the New Testament, he treats passages that mandate disciple-making (Matthew 28:16–20), model the evangelistic practices of Paul (1 Corinthians 9:19–23), describe the role of church leadership and structure (Ephesians 4), and prescribe intergenerational discipleship (Titus 2). Again, though these passages should be applied to the evangelism and discipleship of teenagers, they do not directly support or prove the validity of the institution of student ministry. This chapter runs the risk of overstating its claims. Scripture does describe and prescribe the discipleship of children and youth in the home and in the community of faith. However, the scriptural mandate to disciple teenagers does not require the use of the institution of student ministry to accomplish its mission. Hence the defense of the institution must begin with a firm biblical grounding in the roles of the congregation, the office of overseer, and parents to see the institution continue to benefit churches.

Further, chapter 12 provides a positive bias concerning the historical development of the field of student ministry. Temple finds the historical developments that led to modern youth ministry to be lacking and suggests that only the advent of youth ministry corrected such deficiency. An observation of this development overstates the effectiveness of modern youth ministry and understates the effectiveness of the church prior to the twentieth century. Also, the author does not substantiate his historical claims with any primary sources.

Although there are a few topics that require greater substantiation, overall, *Navigating Student Ministry* will serve student ministers well. The book is largely excellent and should be utilized for the future health of the discipleship culture within a church. Particularly notable are the chapters and appendices authored by Timothy Paul Jones, Paul Kelly, and Karen Jones. Additionally, the volume features worthwhile practical content regarding personal holiness, delegating, qualifications for ministers, disciple-making, evangelizing the lost, and technology.

Equipping Fathers to Lead Family Worship by Kenneth S. Coley and Blair D. Robinson. Nashville, TN: Randall House. 2021. 115 pp. $14.99. paper.

Review by Frank Trimble, director of training and consulting at Family Time Training in Littleton, Colorado.

Kenneth Coley, Ed.D., served Southeastern Baptist Theological Seminary in Wake Forrest, North Carolina, for twenty-five years as a senior professor of Christian Education. He also served as the director of the seminary's Doctor of Education program. He has authored and edited several books, including Teaching for Change: Eight Keys for Transformational Bible Study With Teens (2017). Blair Robinson, D.Min., is the lead pastor of First Baptist Church of Irving, Texas. He previously served as the discipleship pastor of First Irving and as the associate pastor of Christ Covenant Church in Raleigh, North Carolina.

In the present volume, Coley and Robinson offer a guide for pastors to use in equipping fathers to lead family worship in their homes—though the book can also serve fathers directly (p. 3). The book is broken up into three parts. Part one covers the biblical and historical precedent of family worship (chaps. 1–2) as well as provides an overview of the elements of family worship (chap. 3). The biblical precedent chapter offers readers foundational texts that describe or prescribe the practice of family worship and other elements of home discipleship. The chapter on historical precedent lays out early church examples of family worship and explains the emphasis on family worship through the Protestant Reformation, the Puritans, and specific figures such as Richard Baxter and John Knox. The authors do not simply offer accounts of notable historical figures; they also include helpful breakdowns of key teachings from them that can serve fathers today.

In part two, Coley and Robinson provide pastors with practical guidance on how they can equip fathers to prioritize private devotional disciplines (chap. 4), lead their families through key elements of family worship (chaps. 5–6), and model Bible study methods to their families (chap. 7). The authors offer practical guides and breakdowns so that pastors have a palatable way to equip the fathers in their congregations.

Part three concentrates on how pastors can implement the training of fathers and provide continual oversight for them as they lead family worship in their homes. In chapter 8, the authors provide a framework for a four-week training plan in which pastors intentionally train fathers and launch them in the practice of family worship. Chapter 9 is concerned with how pastors can provide accountability and support for the fathers in their congregations. At the end, the authors offer a note of challenge and inspiration directly to fathers.

The book also features three appendices that list helpful resources for further study and cover basic learning concepts.

Coley and Robinson successfully achieve their goal of providing a guide for pastors to equip fathers to lead family worship in their homes while also making the resource accessible for fathers themselves. The size of the book is noteworthy: at 115 pages, the book is a quick read. Further, the authors have produced a resource that is relentlessly practical yet substantive.

For readers who have not been exposed to the biblical and historical precedent for family worship, this book provides an appropriate introduction to the practice while highlighting its importance. At the same time, however, the book is written in an engaging manner; the authors frequently employ personal illustrations and give practical how-to breakdowns for pastors aiming to lead and equip fathers. The book also avoids pretention and assumes nothing about readers' prior knowledge of the subject matter. Hence, this book would be a great fit for any Christian father regardless of his spiritual maturity level.

Out of the book's many strengths, two rise to the surface; its emphasis on the personal holiness of the father and its humble yet firm advocacy of complementarianism (p. 10). Since the book focuses on fathers, it emphasizes their biblical role. The premise of the book illustrates that God has a specific design for what the father is supposed to do vis-à-vis home discipleship. However, throughout the volume, mere ritual is decried, and unhealthy forms of masculinity are nowhere to be found.

In *Equipping Fathers to Lead Family Worship*, Scripture, church history, real experience, and practical instruction undergird Coley and Robinson's mission. This resource would benefit any congregation that is willing to put its principles into practice. Pastors are encouraged to consider implementing a training regimen that resembles what can be found in chapter 8. However, the authors are under no illusion that their approach is the only appropriate method. In short, the book provides a way to be intentional with the equipping (Ephesians 4:11–12) of those who are called to lead their homes. The authors have provided a plan, and readers are left to consider whether or not they will follow it.

The Rise and Triumph of the Modern Self: Cultural Amnesia, Expressive Individualism, and the Road to Sexual Revolution by Carl R. Trueman. Wheaton, IL: Crossway, 2020. 432 pp. $23.00. Hardcover.

Review by Steve Vandegriff, Ed.D., professor, adjunct faculty, and online instructional mentor at Liberty University, Lynchburg, Virginia.

One does not have to look very far, when it comes to current cultural nuances, to discover overt sexual messages that cause most people to shake their head in disbelief. One that has captured the attention of our culture in grandiose fashion is transgenderism. More and more corporations have aligned themselves with this issue, including Adidas, Disney, and Target, to name a few. Even Barbie has her own transgender Barbie doll. This causes many parents and grandparents, along with critical thinkers of faith and practical theology, to ask an important question: Where on earth did this transgender movement come from? Carl Trueman answers that question in *The Rise and Triumph of the Modern Self.*

Carl Trueman, Ph.D., is a professor of biblical and religious studies at Grove City College and is a recognized church historian, as well as a fellow at the Ethics and Public Policy Center. He has authored or edited a number of books. *The Rise and Triumph of the Modern Self* is not only a thorough treatment of the topic, but also extraordinarily timely. To be clear, while timeliness can have the perception that this will become dated sooner than later, that is not the case with this book. This book is timely with regard to the urgency of awareness with Trueman's address, as well as the potential long-term consequences.

Although Trueman engages a subject as diverse as the "sexual revolution," he filters through the LGBTQ+ movement while accentuating the normalization of transgenderism. The author skillfully walks the reader back through history, in order to learn from it. Readers will quickly realize that this is a deep dive, not just into the historicity of sexualized thought and philosophy, but also how these writers and thinkers changed the trajectories of how culture(s) manifested their thoughts and ideas. These writers and thinkers were not just spouting banal words to acquiesce some and placate others. Their intentions were often to create change in cultural thinking, particularly in the context of sexuality, while anticipating the formation of some type of social/political enclave, often at the expense of all things related to Christianity.

Readers will find themselves engulfed in the midst of notable philosophical writers and thinkers (Rousseau, Marx, Nietzsche, Darwin, Freud, to name a few). Trueman introduces readers to philosophers who emphasized psychological and sociological thought. This philosophical evaluation then leads toward the political, for without the political piece, change and acceptance (whether volitionally or not) could not take place. Trueman makes it clear that this outcome is worth a clarion call because what will become politically expedient (the normalization of transgenderism) is the endgame. It should be noted that Trueman does make note of those sexual moorings that our culture still rejects (i.e. pedophilia) but whether one likes to admit it or not (Trueman admits this), even these sexual moorings could be compromised by political oppression that has been swayed simply due to current cultural distaste of the nuclear family.

Before the reader gets too far into Trueman's book, it will become apparent that this book is not a biblical response to a disturbing trend in our sexualized culture. In fact, the reader will only find one reference to the apostle Paul and only one biblical reference, in the book. However, to be a bit editorial, that is by design. Trueman has made it clear that our current cultural way of thinking, specifically on the topic of sexuality, has been shaped by disgruntled and religiously void writers of different generations. Reasoning with Scripture would be futile simply due to its juxtaposition to all things religious. In addition, Trueman also demonstrates that our current culture is anti-historical, which not only means that history is a false narrative and needs revision, but it also demands the "destruction of history and its replacement with nothing of any significant substance" (p. 91).

So where do those people of faith and family go from here? The Epilogues and Prologue are worth the price of this book as Trueman concludes with a word of hope (p. 404) and a call to the church (p. 402–407). It is a call to, as Rod Dreher wrote in his foreword, "find ways to keep the true light of faith burning in this present darkness, which comprehends it not" (p. 13).

Biblical Worldview: What it Is, Why it Matters, and How to Shape the Worldview of the Next Generation by Josh Mulvihill. Renewanation. 2019. 233 pp. $14.54. paper.

Review by Charles Carpenter, Ph.D., who serves as professor of Humanities and dean of students at Texas Baptist College. He has served in Christian Higher Education and in pastoral and campus ministries and has significant experience teaching and coaching in Christian Secondary Education.

In a society known for its shifting definitions and reappropriation of competing ideas about God, family, and work, a reaffirmation of what the Bible says concerning these matters is necessary and warranted. *Biblical Worldview*, by Josh Mulvihill, Ph.D., offers an introductory foundation for leaders (parents, grandparents, church leaders, and academics) to train and equip young people and adult leaders to follow Christ more faithfully, defending their faith and knowing how to use the Scriptures with wisdom.

He argues that one's "ship-wrecked faith" is directly tied to how much one reads, understands, and applies the Scriptures. Because, as he maintains, there is a drift from scriptural meditation and core biblical doctrines, he calls churches, families, and academic institutions to "prioritize discipleship over athletics and academics, and for Christian schools to prioritize maturity in Christ over college prep or academic rigor." Moreover, he writes, concerning his book, "*Biblical Worldview* is a serious call to shape the next generation's beliefs with the Bible." Mulvihill argues, that in order to hold back the tide of shifting definitions and faulty perspectives on foundation matters, leaders must offer a biblical worldview pervasive enough to answer the questions young people face today (e.g. creation, marriage, divorce, Jesus, gender education, abortion, parenting, flat earth, Islam, immigration, and vaccines).

Mulvihill divides his book into three parts, with each part containing about four chapters. The book is about half the height of an average book containing 223 pages with a ten-page appendix, consisting of an annotative bibliography of books and resources that treat specific worldview issues.

In his *Biblical Worldview* text, he stresses the importance of the family to establish a biblical world without diminishing the role of the church or the school. Further, he gives examples where the Bible treats an issue, and how the average Christian fails to know how to apply the clear, reasonable, and logical teaching of Scriptures. Each chapter is an "easy-to-read," "Cliffs-Notes" introduction to a "high-view-of-Scripture" intended to "equip" the Christian leader "to make a real and lasting difference" as he/she stresses the importance of discipleship to establish a pervasive, biblical worldview for young people today.

In "Part 1: Introduction to Biblical Worldview," he establishes the "Why," "What," and "Who" in the establishment of a biblical worldview. Mulvihill directs the reader to the Scriptures to answer each of these interrogative pronouns, recognizing that a proper interpretation and relationship with the Bible assures a good foundation for a Christian worldview. Even before a child can read, Christian leaders must model how the Bible addresses the contemporary issues of the day. This is how Christian leaders train young people "to love God's Word, trust God's Word, and live by God's Word." He reminds the reader that "A child's belief system, his or her worldview, is almost fully formed by the age of twelve." It is for this reason that everyone, "parents, other family members, typically grandparents, teachers and coaches, friends and pastors or religious leaders," is vital in passing on a Christian worldview to the next generation.

This vital group of people are those who are to model and teach the importance and implementation of a Christian worldview. The implementation of a Christian worldview begins with the establishment of a biblical framework for addressing challenging issues. For Mulvihill the biblical framework has four main parts: Creation, Rebellion, Salvation, and Restoration. Answering these four truths from the Scriptures allow children to be "rooted and built up in Christ" and gives them a starting point for good Bible interpretation.

In "Part 2: The Biblical Foundation," he offers a guide to help young people establish a way to understand the Scriptures in order to "Develop a love for the Bible." For children to grow up to a maturity in Christ and develop a love for the Scriptures, Mulvihill contends, he/she must find ways to apply the Bible in the proclamation of "the gospel, communicating wisdom [and] warning, teaching the Bible, … asking questions, testimony telling, communicating a blessing, ... prayer, [and] memorizing ... the Bible." As a young person prioritizes the message of and the meditation on the Scriptures, he/she will trust in the "authority," "sufficiency," and "efficacy" of God's Truth.

Even though Mulvihill centralizes on the priority of the Scriptures itself, he offers some helpful resources and guides to address current challenges to laying a good foundation to become "mighty in the Scriptures." He encourages reading the Bible inductively and having a basic commentary, Bible dictionary, concordance, and Bible Atlas to aid in proper examination of the biblical text. Additionally, he encourages the biblical student to frame questions about biblical themes in a way for Christians to know how the Bible is consistent and reliable. He does this by using a series of charts that address key ideas and biblical passages which address central themes. Colossians 2 is the foundation for these key ideas, which, for Mulvihill, is a guide "to receive Christ," "walk in His way," ... [and] become "deeply rooted in the faith." Using Colossians as a guide he lays a foundation "to offer a good [worldview] ... and drive out bad" ones.

In "Part 3: The Bible's Big Story," he articulates the main doctrines which shape the Scriptures and one's biblical understanding of the world and eternity. With this section, he seeks to ward off narrow worldviews which relegates the Bible to specific areas of conversion, life, and application. Mulvihill writes, "many homes, churches, and schools only teach a narrow worldview that is limited to rebellion and salvation but does not concern itself with the broader Christian life and thinking." He illustrates how non-biblical worldviews counterfeit and mask what the Bible offers as "the true account of history from the beginning of time until eternity." The truthful account of the Scriptures offers a unity from the beginning with creation and ending with restoration. Deviating from this account of Scripture leads to one buying into the counterfeits like evolution, relativism, humanism, secularism, socialism, moralism, and Islam.

For Mulvihill, the pervasive message of the gospel is not only how a single biblical passage addresses a particular issue or how many passages deal with a central doctrine, but also the thematic principle that begins with creation and ends with restoration. This thematic principle addresses competing worldviews like Marxism, Hinduism, Socialism, and Islam. This pervasive message begins with personal salvation; personal salvation is not the only goal for a Christian. For Mulvihill, personal salvation is the starting point from which one can treat difficult worldview issues. Mulvihill explains how salvation "is the answer for sin," but the Gospel mandates the believer to restore and reconcile the world back to God through the pervasive message of Christ and His work. Even though this pervasive message begins with a personal, even private repentance, and faith unto salvation, one's "faith belongs in the public arena of education, politics, social media, and the workplace."

The pervasive message of the Gospel and the grounding of Scripture is the strength of Mulvihill's work. He challenges leaders to address every issue with the Gospel in mind and the tools of the Scripture. Moreover, before he closes each chapter, he directs leaders to asking probing questions while addressing particular passages of Scripture. In several places, he summarizes the key beliefs of a competing worldview while briefly explaining how the particular worldview directly opposes a biblical worldview. Even though these are strengths of the book, they are its weaknesses as well. Summarizing a competing worldview, the way he does, makes the particular worldview seem trite, superficial, and inane. This off-handed approach could lead to arrogance and limited understanding of one's worldview. Similarly, he suggests that there are simple and singular answers to difficult issues like marriage, vaccinations, schooling, and the like. It would be helpful for Mulvihill to at least offer a footnote or a sentence occasionally showing that good, biblical, and wise Christians wrestle with these issues, and if one differs from the other, the one should not characterize the other as having a non-biblical worldview.

In conclusion, Mulvihill's work is needed and helpful as a primer to worldview thinking. He encourages believers to think reasonably and pervasively about the Scriptures and how they address social and cultural issues.

For the Faith of the Next Generation: A Resource for Ministry Leaders and Parents by Julie Kurz with Scott Turansky, Joanne Miller, Carri Taylor, and Kirk Weaver. Nashville, TN: D6 Family Ministry. 2022. 262 pp. $24.99. paper.

Review by Jeff Nichols who is the current state director for Child Evangelism Fellowship of Tennessee, assuming that role after 25+ years on staff at The Donelson Fellowship in Nashville, Tennessee. He is a former children's pastor, youth pastor, and executive pastor with 30+ years of ministry experience who loves his kids, his grandkids, and kids all around the world.

> I could not help but ask myself if there was more we could do in children's ministries. Why, after years of being in Sunday School, learning about God's plan for their lives and seemingly making commitments to follow Jesus, couldn't we keep our children from falling away in such spectacular fashion?

With this piercing question on page one of the Introduction, Julie Kurz lays out a problem she has spent years trying to answer. And she is not new to this struggle. With more than 30 years of experience in children's ministry as a children's ministry director, consultant, coach, and a children's ministry specialist for Church Assistance Ministries, she knows well the joys, struggles, and challenges of ministry leaders and parents. Kurz launched Reconnect Ministries in 2006 with the express purpose of establishing a biblical model for passing faith to the next generation. This model recognizes the home as the primary source of spiritual development for children and sees the church as coming alongside parents, not replacing them.

Kurz notes that her writing style is meant to be more like a letter to a dear friend than a book. This book does read more like a letter than a dissertation and her casual writing style is an easy read. As she explores a wide range of topics related to answering the big question asked in the introduction, she deals with the hard facts and statistics that show the preferred method of reaching children over the last few decades has not had the desired effect or impact on those children when they grow older in life or in faith.

She relates examples of her years of experience in children's ministry to support this premise. Kurz has developed ministry strategies with specific spiritual targets, then ministered within that setting long enough to evaluate whether or not the target was hit. A realization came to her when she was confronted with the fact that many of the children who had grown up in her ministry were not attending church when they got to high school. This made her ask, "Could I really be responsible for the spiritual foundation of children growing up in our church?"

This refrain occurs over and over throughout the book as she dealt with the reality of the limited influence a few hours a week at church can have on children. This kind of honest examination sheds a light on a weakness of the current methodologies and approaches to ministry that she is not afraid to address. The book peels back the layers that have contributed to this current state of affairs, but it also provides plenty of assistance for anyone wanting to do something about it.

One of the most amazing benefits of reading this book is the list of resources referenced and cited throughout the book. Many books will refer to a source that has served as mental fodder to arrive at a certain conclusion, but Kurz does more. Throughout the book she will not only refer to another source but give a summary of the key thought that served to push her in her thinking about a certain topic or issue. Seldom do you buy a book just for the bibliography, but this may be the exception. The reader is the recipient of the overflow of vast reading by Kurz. She even allows subject matter experts in fields such as heart-based approach to parenting, family time devotions, and the impact of divorce and remarriage on the family to write entire chapters on their subjects. Turansky, Miller, Weaver, and Taylor provide clear insight in these areas which are important factors in constructing a ministry to children that is parent-partner focused.

While not an exhaustive list of all that is covered in the last half of the book a few themes occur over and over, such as:

- The need to teach children the Bible as one story, as one book. She gives a good list of curriculum publishers that have taken this approach in their teaching material. Again, Kurz is a fount of good suggestions on where to find valuable resources.

- How to avoid "performance-driven" faith.
- Is salvation an event or a journey? This question is considered from several different angles as Kurz wrestles with the age-old challenge of children's ministry—how to lead children to Christ without making it about a moment in time at a big event. This is a valuable exercise for any parent or children's ministry leader to work through as they consider how they want to guide children who want to place a saving faith in Christ.

This book is a worthy read by anyone wanting to take the responsibility of spiritually shepherding children seriously.

Big Things Start Small: How Small Groups Helped Ignite Christianity's Greatest Spiritual Awakenings by Joe M. Easterling. Eugene, OR: Wipf & Stock, 2021. 196 pp. $25.00. Paperback or eBook. $40.00. Hardcover.

Review by Jerry Calvin McKinney, Ed.D., who serves as adjunctive professor of Christian Education and administrator for the Doctor of Education Studies Office at Southeastern Baptist Theological Seminary in Wake Forest, North Carolina.

Joe Easterling gives a robust review of the history of church revivals from the time of biblical writings, through the Reformational period, into the Great Awakenings during the early development of the United States, and into the more modern revivals of the 20th Century. This survey of revivals focuses on those taking place in the United States but launches from a historical viewpoint tracing the major events in Western world history. Easterling brings a fresh wind to the topic of revival as he sweeps through a review of some of the great names in modern church history.

Joe M. Easterling, Ph.D., serves as assistant professor at the Liberty University School of Divinity in Lynchburg, Virginia, and also as discipleship pastor at Northside Church in Wilmington, North Carolina, where his wife and two daughters are also members. *Big Things Start Small* is his first published book that emerged from his research while pursuing a second doctoral degree. Easterling's research provides a launching pad for students interested in learning about small groups and their impact upon the advancement of the kingdom, especially here in the United States.

In Chapter 1, he covers small groups in Scripture and the early days of the church when house churches were common. Easterling writes, "The house-church model was so successful during the New Testament time that virtually every instance in the book of Acts of a local church meeting refers to the gathering being in someone's home" (p. 13). He goes on to give a detailed rationale for this New Testament style of worshipping Yahweh as it morphed into the love (agape) feasts that are described in the writings of Paul.

In Chapter 2, Easterling launches from the small group practices of the early church into the impact that small groups had on the Reformation. Here he covers the stories of great names like Waldo, Wycliffe, Huss, and Luther. He then contrasts them with the Anabaptists who "centered on the doctrine of baptism" (p. 41) to distinguish themselves from other groups.

In Chapters 3–6, he shares the development of small group formation that led up to each of the four Great Awakenings, examining the socio-economic, religious, and moral conditions, and how these small groups helped to sustain the effects of the revivals from one to the next. Easterling's treatment of the spread of revival across college campuses makes an interesting undercurrent in his argument. From college campuses to camp meetings and Sunday school, young people feature strongly in the great moves of God throughout the United States, Wales, and Korea. Notably, Campus Crusade for Christ, the Jesus People Movement, and coffeehouses became primary foci for spreading the revival spirit across the land.

At the end of their respective chapters, Easterling provides tables showcasing key observations of the catalytic small groups during each of the four major awakenings. He wraps up his book with an epilogue that ends with a table summarizing small group features, leaders, and proponents among other interesting observations. These data tables give helpful snapshots of Easterling's data gathering and conclusions, thus making it easier for the reader to follow along with his argument.

Easterling concludes with six small group features for igniting the flames of revival again: Focus on studying the Bible; Focus on praying;

Focus on discipleship & holiness; Focus on worshipping with music; Allow gatherings to overflow into culture; And focus on transformational awakening instead of logistics.

While Easterling paints a historically accurate portrayal of the role of small groups in catalyzing revivals throughout American history, he stops just short of speaking to the many moves of God that have happened since the Mid-Century Revival (1949–1979). With more than 40 years of current church history in the United States. left untouched, Easterling leaves the door open to writing another book that could follow up on more recent developments in various denominations across the Unites States. Furthermore, he could expand his research to speak to the impacts of small groups on revivals that are currently occurring in many places across the earth.

The Biggest Story Bible Storybook: 104 Engaging Bible Stories for Ages 6–12 by Kevin DeYoung (Illustrated by Don Clark) Wheaton, IL: Crossway. 2022. 528 pp. $21.43. hardcover/dustjacket.

Review by Tony A. Rogers, D.Min., senior pastor of Southside Baptist Church in Bowie Texas. Tony also serves as the executive director of Jeremiah 20:9 Ministries in Bowie Texas.

Kevin DeYoung and Don Clark provide an invaluable service to both the home and the church with this treasure-trove of child-friendly Bible stories. DeYoung (Ph.D., University of Leicester) is the author and serves as both pastor (Christ Covenant Church, Matthews, North Carolina), and professor (Reformed Theological Seminary, Charlotte, North Carolina). He and his wife Trisha have nine children. Clark (cofounder of Invisible Creature) serves as illustrator and is an award-winning artist. He and his wife, Erika are the parents of three and live in Seattle, Washington. These are stories from God's Word designed for ages 6–12, but parents will certainly enjoy this work as well.

DeYoung introduces this collection with insightful "Notes to Parents" (pp. 10–11). He informs readers that this "is a story book about the Bible, but it is not the Bible ... if you have to choose between reading the Bible or reading this book, by all means read the Bible" (p. 10). He defines his parameters, "Although I've tried hard not to take creative blessings with the text of Scripture, I've not simply repeated it either. What you have in this book is our theologically minded and redemptively focused interpretation of the main stories in the Bible" (p. 10). He offers advice to those who participate in this undertaking, "allow time for spontaneous questions, to ask good questions, to talk about the pictures, and to discuss not just what of the story but the why, the how, and the Who" (p. 11).

One hundred and four theological adaptions unfold in seven sections: Part 1: The Pentateuch (Genesis-Deuteronomy 20 stories), Part 2: History (Joshua-Esther 16 stories), Part 3: Poetry (Job-Song of Solomon 4 stories), Part 4: the Prophets (Isaiah-Malachi 12 stories), Part 5: the Gospels (Matthew-John 32 stories), Part 6: Acts and the Epistles (Acts-Jude 16 stories), and Part 7: Revelation (4 stories). These chapters are not intended to stand alone but are meant to reveal the grand narrative of Scripture from Genesis to Revelation framed in a kid-friendly way. Each story ends with a prayer that is applicably grounded in that story. The artwork is captivating, and the authors are aware of the inherent dangers of bringing the words of Scripture to life with the corresponding designs. This is especially true in the presentation of Jesus. The author and illustrator sought to be neither culturally unrealistic, cartoonish, or idolatrous; instead, they simply present the main character artistically stylized as opposed to silhouettes and shadows (p. 11).

This book presents several positive features. First, DeYoung ably places theology on the lower shelf where children can reach it with such gems as, "Although the Lord loved the world He had made, He didn't love how worldly it had become" (p. 34) or "After twenty years, Jacob was starting to change. Because God's promises were not" (p. 73). One of the most rewarding sections is the "Snake Crusher is Crushed for Us" (Mark 15) (pp. 418–425).

Second, the book indelibly etches phrases, titles, and concepts on the mind. Phrases like, "Every other hero is a mixed bag—like a sack full of jelly beans and baby carrots" (p. 128) or "the fruit of the off-limits tree" (p. 26) or the "live-forever tree" (p. 30). Scintillating are The Miraculous Catnap (Daniel 6) (pp. 244–249) and modernizing Psalm 23 to rhyme (p. 208).

Next, sometimes conveying death to children can be challenging. The authors are commended for doing so truthfully without being gratuitous, still being faithful to the sacred text (e.g., Red Sea swallowing up the Egyptians [pp. 90–91], John the Baptist beheaded [p. 338], death of Sapphira and Ananias [pp. 450–453], and the depiction of Hell [pp. 520–521]).

Lastly, if a picture is worth a thousand words, then Clark's illustrations speak volumes, especially his depictions of Noah (pp. 36–39), Sodom and Gomorrah (pp. 60–61), Elijah's chariot of fire (pp. 170–171), Ezekiel's valley of dry bones (pp. 227–231), and the Holy City that John saw (p. 525).

This volume will alter your family altar and serve well in several church settings. This edition serves as a vital addition to the *Biggest Story Suite* featuring *The Biggest Story: How the Snake Crusher Brings Us Back to the Garden* (Crossway, 2015); *The Biggest Story: The Animated Short Film* (Crossway, 2016); and *The Biggest Story ABC* board book (Crossway, 2017). "When the best stories are told for children—in their idiom and at their level—they are still captivating for adults. They teach children and adults at the same time. I'd love for this book to do the same" (p. 11). DeYoung and Clark rightly perceive that Jesus is the Biggest Story—the theme, goal, and good news, (p. 13) and they are always pointing to Him. They are not seeking to replace Scripture, rather they are providing yet another means to do what the great hymnwriter Fanny Crosby longed for: "Tell me the story of Jesus, write on my heart every word; tell me the story most precious, sweetest that ever was heard."

D6 FAMILY MINISTRY Journal

VOLUME 1 - 2016

ARTICLES

PRACTITIONER INSIGHTS

RANDALL HOUSE
ACADEMIC

For Further information about this journal please go to D6family.com/d6-academic

D6 FAMILY MINISTRY Journal

VOLUME 2 - 2017

ARTICLES

PRACTITIONER INSIGHTS

RANDALL HOUSE
ACADEMIC

D6

FAMILY MINISTRY Journal

VOLUME 3 - 2018

ARTICLES

PRACTITIONER INSIGHTS

RANDALL HOUSE
ACADEMIC

D6

FAMILY MINISTRY

Journal

VOLUME 4 - 2019

ARTICLES

PRACTITIONER INSIGHTS

RANDALL HOUSE
ACADEMIC

For Further information about this journal please go to D6family.com/d6-academic

CPSIA information can be obtained
at www.ICGtesting.com
Printed in the USA
JSHW031146240223
38115JS00002B/5

9 781614 841586